THE POCKET REFERENCE

Herbert Schildt

Osborne **McGraw-Hill**
Berkeley, California

Osborne **McGraw-Hill**
2600 Tenth Street
Berkeley, California 94710
U.S.A.

For information on translations and book distributors outside of
the U.S.A., please write to Osborne **McGraw-Hill** at the above
address.

C: The Pocket Reference

1234567890 SPCO 89876

ISBN 0-07-881321-2

CONTENTS

INTRODUCTION

C was invented and first implemented by Dennis Ritchie on a DEC PDP-11, using the UNIX operating system. C is the result of a development process that started with an older language called BCPL, which is still in use (primarily in Europe), and was developed by Martin Richards. BCPL influenced a language called B, which was invented by Ken Thompson and which led to the development of C.

For many years, the de facto standard for C was the one supplied with the UNIX version 5 operating system and described in *The C Programming Language* by Brian Kernighan and Dennis Ritchie (Prentice-Hall, 1978). It is often referred to as the "K&R standard." With the popularity of microcomputers, a large number of C implementations were created. In what could almost be called a miracle, most of these implementations were highly compatible with each other on the source code level. However, because no standard existed, there were discrepancies. To alter this situation, a committee was formed in summer 1983 to create an ANSI standard that would define the C language once and for all. As of this writing, the proposed standard is very nearly complete, and its adoption by ANSI is expected in 1987. This pocket reference covers both the ANSI and the K&R standards.

DATA TYPES AND VARIABLES

C has a very rich assortment of built-in data types available to the programmer. In addition, custom data types may be created to fit virtually any need.

BASIC TYPES

C has five basic built-in data types:

Type	C Keyword Equivalent
character	char
integer	int
floating point	float
double floating point	double
valueless	void

All these types (except for **void**) may be modified through the use of the C-type modifiers:

signed   unsigned   short   long

DECLARING VARIABLES

Variable names are strings of letters from one to several characters in length; the maximum length depends on your compiler. For clarity, the underscore may also be used as part of the variable name, such as **first_time**. In C, uppercase and lowercase are different. For example, **test** and **TEST** are two different variables.

All variables must be declared prior to use. The general form of the declaration is:

type variable_name;

For example, to declare **x** to be a float, **y** to be an integer, and **ch** to be a character, you would type:

```
float x;
int y;
char ch;
```

STRUCTURES

A structure is a collection of variables that are grouped and referenced under one name. The general form of a structure declaration is:

```
struct struct_name {
    element 1;
    element 2;
      .
      .
      .
} struct_variable;
```

For example, the following structure has two elements: **name,** a character array, and **balance,** a floating-point number.

```
struct client {
    char name[80];
    float balance;
} list;
```

The dot operator is used to reference individual structure elements if the structure is global or declared in the function referencing it. The arrow operator is used in all other cases. For example, this accesses the **balance** element of **list**.

```
list.balance
```

UNIONS

When two or more variables share the same memory, then a **union** is defined. The general form for a **union** is:

```
union union_name {
    element 1;
    element 2;
      .
      .
      .
} union_variable;
```

The elements of a **union** overlay each other. For example:

```
union tom {
    char ch;
    int x;
} t;
```

declares a **union t** that looks like this in memory:

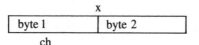

The individual variables that comprise the **union** are referenced using the dot operator. The arrow operator is used with a pointer to a **union**.

ENUMERATIONS

Another type of variable that can be created is called an *enumeration*. An enumeration is essentially a list of objects (or values, depending upon how you think about it). As such, an enumeration type is simply a specification of the list of objects that belong to the enumeration. When a variable is declared to be of an enumeration type, then its only values may be those defined by the enumeration.

To create an enumeration requires the use of the keyword **enum**. The general form of an enumeration type is:

```
enum name { list of values };
```

For example, the following short program defines an enumeration of cities called **cities** and the variable **c** of type **cities**. Finally, the program will assign **c** the value "Houston."

```
enum cities {Houston, Austin, Amarillo };
enum cities c;
main()
{
    c = Houston;
}
```

STORAGE CLASS TYPE MODIFIERS

The type modifiers **extern**, **auto**, **register**, **const**, **volatile**, and **static** are used to alter the way C creates storage for the following variables:

extern: If the **extern** modifier is placed before a variable name, the compiler will know that that variable has been declared elsewhere. The **extern** modifier is most commonly used when there are two or more files sharing the same global variables.

auto: An **auto** variable is created upon entry into a block and destroyed upon exit. For example, all variables defined inside a function are **auto** by default. Although **auto** variables are seldom used, they can be valuable as specialized or dedicated systems where RAM is in short supply.

register: The **register** modifier can only be used on local integer or character variables. It causes the compiler to attempt to keep that value in a register of the CPU instead of placing it in memory. This makes all references to that variable extremely fast.

For example, the following function uses a **register** variable for loop control:

```
f1()
{
    register int t;
    for(t = 0;t<10000; + +t) {
    .
    .
    .
    }
}
```

const: Variables of type **const** may not be changed by your program during execution. The compiler is free to place variables of this type into read-only-memory (ROM). For example:

```
const int a;
```

will create an integer called **a** that may not be modified by your program. It can, however, be used in other types of expressions. A **const** variable will receive its value either from an explicit initialization or by some hardware-dependent means. Including **const**-type variables aids in the development of ROM-able applications.

volatile: The modifier **volatile** is used to tell the compiler that a variable's value may be changed in ways not explicitly specified by the program. For example, a global variable's address may be passed to the clock routine of the operating system and used to hold the realtime of the system. In this situation, the contents of the variable are altered without any explicit assignment statements in the program. This is important because some C compilers will automatically optimize certain expressions by assuming that the contents of a variable do not change inside that expression, in order to achieve higher performance. The **volatile** modifier will prevent this optimization.

static: You can add the modifier **static** to any of the basic data types. The **static** modifier instructs the C compiler to keep a local variable in existence during the lifetime of the program instead of creating and destroying it. The values of local variables are discarded when a function finishes and returns. Using **static** maintains their value between function calls.

ADDRESSING TYPE MODIFIERS

Many C compilers designed for use with the 8086 family of processors have added the following modifers. These may be applied to pointer declarations to allow explicit control—and override—of the default-addressing mode used to compile your program.

_cs	_ds	_es	_ss
far	near	huge	

The 8086 uses a segmented memory architecture with a

total address space of one megabyte. However, this one megabyte is divided into 64K *segments*. The 8086 can directly access any byte with a segment and does so with a 16-bit register. Therefore, the address of any specific byte within the computer is the combination of the segment number and the 16-bit address.

The 8086 uses four segments: one for code, one for data, one for stack, and one extra segment. All segments must start on addresses that are even multiples of 16.

To calculate the actual byte referred to by the combination of the segment and offset, first shift the value in the segment register to the left by 4 bits and then add in the offset. This makes a 20-bit address. For example, if the segment register holds the value 10H and the offset 100H, then the following sequence shows how the actual address is derived.

segment register: 0000 0000 0001 0000

segment shifted: 0000 0001 0000 0000

offset: 0000 0001 0000 0000

segment + offset: 0000 0010 0000 0000 (200H)

In the 8086, addresses are most commonly referred to in *segment:offset* form. In this form, the outcome of the foregoing example is 0010:0100H.

There are many segment:offsets that can describe the same byte because the segments may overlap each other. For example, 0000:0010 is the same as 0001:0000.

The 8086 only requires a 16-bit address to access memory within the segment already loaded into one of its segment registers. However, if you wish to access memory outside that segment, then both the segment register and the offset must be loaded with the proper values. This effectively means that a 32-bit address is required. The difference between the two is that it takes twice as long to load two 16-bit registers as it does to load one, hence your programs run much slower. The exact way they run slower is determined by the memory model used by the program.

Most C compilers for the 8086 family of processors can compile your program six different ways, and each way organizes the memory in the computer a different way. The six models are called tiny, small, medium, compact, large, and huge.

Tiny Model: The tiny model compiles a C program so that all the segment registers are set to the same value and all addressing is done using 16-bits. This means that the code, data, and stack must all be within the same 64K segment. This method of compilation produces the smallest, fastest code. Programs compiled using this version may be converted into ".COM" files using the DOS command "EXE2BIN".

Small Model: In the small model, all addressing is done using only the 16-bit offset. The code segment is separate from the data, stack, and extra segments, which are in their own segment. This means that the total size of a program compiled this way is 128K, split between code and data. The addressing time is the same as that for the tiny model, but the program can be twice as big.

Medium Model: The medium model is for large programs where the code exceeds the one-segment restriction of the small model. Here, the code may use multiple segments and requires 32- bit pointers. However, the stack, data, and extra segments are in their own segment and use 16-bit address. This is good for large programs that use little data.

Compact Model: The complement of the medium model is the compact model. In this version, program code is restricted to one segment but data may occupy several segments. This means that all accesses to data require 32-bit addressing but the code uses 16-bit addressing. This is good for programs that require large amounts of data but little code.

Large Model: The large model allows both code and data to use multiple segments. However, the largest single item of data, such as an array, is limited to 64K. This model is used when you have both large code and data requirements. It also runs much slower than any of the previous versions.

Huge Model: The huge model is the same as the large model, except that individual data items may exceed 64k. This makes runtime speed degrade further.

Overriding a Memory Model: The addressing modifiers may only be applied to pointers or to functions. When applied to pointers they affect the way data is accessed. When applied to functions, they affect the way the function is called and returned from.

The address modifier follows the base type and precedes the variable name. For example, this declares a **far** pointer called **f_pointer**.

```
char far *f_pointer;
```

When an address modifier is used, it causes the compiler to use the specified addressing mode rather than the default mode.

ARRAYS

You may declare arrays of any data type. The general form of a singly dimensioned array is:

```
type var-name[size];
```

where *size* specifies the number of elements in the array. For example, to declare an integer array **x** of 100 elements you would write:

```
int x[100];
```

This will create an array that is 100 elements long, with the first element being 0 and the last being 99. For example, the following loop will load the numbers 0 through 99 into array **x**:

```
for(t=0;t<100; t++) x[t]=t;
```

Multidimensional arrays are declared by placing the additional dimensions inside additional brackets.

FUNCTIONS

A C program is a collection of one or more user-defined functions. One of the functions must be called **main** because execution will begin at this function. Traditionally, **main**() is the first function in a program; however, it could go anywhere in the program.

The general form of a C function is:

```
type function_name(parameter list)
parameter declaration
{
    body of function
}
```

If the function has no parameters, then no parameter declaration is needed. The type declaration is optional— if no explicit type declaration is present, the function defaults to integer. Functions terminate and return automatically to the calling procedure when the last brace is encountered. You may force a return prior to that by using the **return** statement.

All functions, except those declared as **void**, return a value. The type of the return value must match the type declaration of the function. If no explicit type declaration has been made, then the return value is defaulted to integer. If a **return** statement is part of the function, then the value of the function is the value in the **return** statement. If no **return** is present, then the function will return zero.

If a function is going to return a value other than integer, then its type must reflect this fact. Also, it will be necessary to declare the function prior to any reference to it by another piece of code. This can best be done by making a function declaration in the global definition area of the program. The following example shows how the function **fn**() is declared to return a floating point value.

```
float fn();
main()
{
.
.
.
printf("%f", fn());
.
.
.
}
float fn()
{
return 12.23;
}
```

Because all functions except those declared as **void** have a value, they may be used in any arithmetic statement. For example, beginning C programmers tend to write code like:

```
x = sqrt(y);
z = sin(x);
```

whereas a more experienced programmer would write:

```
z = sin(sqrt(y));
```

SCOPE AND LIFETIME OF VARIABLES

C has two general classes of variables: *global* and *local*. A global variable is available for use by all functions in the program, while a local variable is known and used only by the function in which it is declared. In some C literature, global variables are refered to as *external* variables and local variables are called *dynamic* or *automatic* variables. This pocket reference uses the terms local and global because they are more commonly used.

A global variable must be declared outside of all functions, including the **main()** function. Global variables are generally placed at the top of the file, prior to **main()**, for ease of reading and because a variable must be declared before it is used. A local variable is declared inside a function after the function's opening brace. For example, the following program declares one global, **x**, and two local variables, **x** and **y**.

```c
int x;
main()
{
    int y;
    y = f1();
    x = 100;
    printf("%d %d", x, x*y);
}
f1()
{
    int x;
    scanf("%d", &x);
    return x;
}
```

This program will multiply the number entered from the keyboard by 100. Please note that the local variable **x** in **f1()** has no relationship to the global variable **x**. This is because local variables that have the same name as global variables always take precedence over the global ones.

Global variables stay in existence the entire duration of the program, while local variables are created when the function is entered and destroyed when the function is exited. This means that local variables do not hold their values between function calls. You can use the **static** modifier, however, to preserve values between calls.

The formal parameters to a function are also local variables and, aside from their job of receiving the value of the calling arguments, behave and can be used like any other local variable.

MAIN FUNCTION

All C programs must have a **main()** function. When execution begins, this is the first function that is called. You must not have more than one function called **main()**.

When **main()** terminates, the program is over and control passes back to the operating system.

The only parameters that are allowed to **main()** are **argc** and **argv**. These two variables will hold the number of command line arguments and a character pointer to them, respectively. Command line arguments are the information that you type in after the program name when you execute a program. For example, when you compile a C program, you type something like this: CC MYPROG.C—where MYPROG.C is the name of the program you wish to compile and is a command line argument. **argc** will always be at least one because the program name is the first argument as far as C is concerned. **argv** must be declared as an array of character pointers. The use is shown here in a short program that will print your name on the screen.

```
main(argc, argv)
int argc;
char *argv[];
{
    if(argc<2)
        printf("enter your name on the command
        line./n");
    else
        printf("hello %s/n",argv[1]);
}
```

Notice that **argv** is delcared as a character pointer array of unknown size. The C compiler will automatically determine the size of the array necessary to handle all the command line arguments.

C STANDARD LIBRARY

C does not have built-in functions to perform disk I/O, console I/O, and a number of other useful procedures. These things are accomplished in C by using a set of predefined library functions that are supplied with the compiler. This library is usually called the *C Standard Library*.

OPERATORS

C has a very rich set of operators, which can be divided into the following classes: arithmetic, relational and logical, bitwise, pointer, assignment, and miscellaneous.

ARITHMETIC OPERATORS

C has the following seven arithmetic operators:

Operator	Action
−	subtraction, unary minus
+	addition
*	multiplication
/	division
%	modulo division
− −	decrement
+ +	increment

The **+, -, *** and / operators work in the expected fashion. The % operator returns the remainder of an integer division. The increment and decrement operators increase or decrease the operand by one.

The precedence of these operators is:

highest	+ + − − − (unary minus)
	* / %
lowest	+ −

Operators on the same precedence level are evaulated left to right.

RELATIONAL AND LOGICAL OPERATORS

The relational and logical operators are used to produce TRUE/FALSE results and are often used together. In C, *any* non-zero number evaluates TRUE. However, a C relational or logical expression produces the number 1 for TRUE and 0 for FALSE. The relational and logical operators are listed here:

Relational Operator	Meaning
>	greater than
> =	greater than or equal
<	less than
< =	less than or equal
= =	equal
! =	not equal
Logical Operator	**Meaning**
&&	AND
||	OR
!	NOT

The relational operators are used to compare two values. The logical operators are used to connect two values or, in the case of the NOT, to reverse the value of a value. The precedence of these operators is:

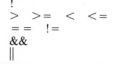

highest   !
                   >   >=   <   <=
                   ==   !=
                   &&
lowest   \|\|

As an example, the following **if** statement evaluates TRUE and prints the line **X is less than 10**:

```
X = 9;
if(X < 10) printf("X is less than 10");
```

However, in the next example no message is displayed because both operands associated with the AND must be true for the outcome to be true.

```
X = 9;
Y = 9;
if(X < 10 && Y > 10) printf("X is less than 10; Y is greater");
```

THE BITWISE OPERATORS

Unlike most other programming languages, C provides operators that manipulate the actual bits inside a variable. The bitwise operators can only be used on integers or characters. These operators are:

Bitwise Operator	Meaning
&	AND
|	OR
^	XOR
~	One's complement
>>	right shift
<<	left shift

AND, OR, and XOR: The truth tables for the AND, OR and XOR are:

&	0	1		|	0	1		^	0	1
0	0	0		0	0	1		0	0	1
1	0	1		1	1	1		1	1	0

These rules are applied to each bit in a byte when the bitwise AND, OR, and XOR operations are performed.

In a program, you use the &, | and | like any other operator, as shown here:

```
main()
{
    char x,y,z;
    x = 1; y = 2; z = 4;
    x = x & y; /* x now equals zero */
    y = x | z; /* y now equals 4 */
}
```

The One's Complement Operator: The one's complement operator, ~, will invert all the bits in a byte. For example, if a character variable, **ch**, has the bit pattern:

    0011 1001

then

    ch = ~ch;

places the bit pattern

    1100 0110

into **ch**.

The Shift Operators: The right and left shift operators

19

shift all bits in a byte or a word the specified amount. As bits are shifted, zeros are brought in. The number on the right side of the shift operator specifies the number of positions to shift. The general form of each shift operator is:

variable >> number of bit positions
variable << number of bit positions

Given this bit pattern: 0011 1101, a shift right yields 0001 1110 while a shift left produces 0111 1010.

A shift right is effectively a division by 2, and a shift left is a multiplication by 2. The following code fragment will first multiply and then divide the value in **x**.

```
int x;
x = 10;
x = x<<1;
x = x>>1;
```

Because of how negative numbers are represented inside the machine, be careful when trying to use a shift for multiplication or division. Moving a 1 into the most significant bit position will make the computer think that the 1 is a negative number.

The precedence of the bitwise operators is:

highest   ~

                         >>   <<

                         &

                         ^

lowest |

POINTER OPERATORS

The two pointer operators are * and &. It is unfortunate that these operators use the same symbols as the multiplication operator and the bitwise AND, since they have nothing in common with them.

The & Pointer Operator: The **&** operator returns the address of the variable it precedes. For example, if the integer **x** is located at memory address 1000, then

```
y = &x;
```

places the value 1000 into **y**. The & can be thought of as "the address of." For example, the previous statement could be read as "place the address of x into y."

The * Pointer Operator: The * operator takes the value of the variable it precedes and uses that value as the address of the information in memory. For example,

```
y = &x;
*y = 100;
```

places the value 100 into **x**. The * can be remembered as "at address". This example could be read as, "place the value 100 at address y". The * operator can also be used on the right-hand side of an assignment. For example,

```
y = &x;
*y = 100;
z = *y/10;
```

places the value of 10 into **z**.

void Pointers: A pointer of type **void** is said to be a generic pointer and can be used to point to any type of object. This implies that pointers of any type can be assigned to pointers of type **void** and vice versa by using the appropriate type casts. To declare a **void** pointer, use a declaration similar to: void *p

The **void** pointer is particularly useful when various types of pointers will be manipulated by a single routine.

ASSIGNMENT OPERATORS

In C, the assignment operator is the single equals sign. However, C allows a very convenient form of "shorthand" for assignments of the general type:

```
variable1 = variable1 operator expression;
```

For example:

```
x = x + 10;
y = y/z;
```

Assignments of this type can be shortened to:

variable1 operator = expression;

or, specifically in the case of the examples above,

```
x + = 10;
y/ = z;
```

THE ? OPERATOR

The ? operator is a ternary operator that is used to replace if statements of the folowing general type:

```
if expression1 then x = expression2
else x = expression2
```

The general form of the ? operator is:

variable = expression1 ? expression2 : expression3;

If expression1 is TRUE, then the value assigned is that of expression2; otherwise it is the value of expression3. For example:

```
x = (y<10) ? 20 : 40;
```

will assign **x** the value of 20 if **y** is less than 10, and 40 if it is not.

The reason that this operator exists, beyond saving typing, is that a C compiler can produce very efficient code for this statement—much faster than the similar **if/else** statement.

STRUCTURE AND UNION OPERATORS

The . (dot) operator and the –> (arrow) operator are used to reference individual elements of structures and unions. The dot operator is applied to the actual structure or union. The arrow operator is used with a pointer to a structure or a union. For example, given the global structure:

```
struct date_time {
    char date[16];
    int time;
} tm;
```

to assign the value "3/12/88" to element **date** of structure **tm**, you would write

    strcpy(tm.date, "3/12/88");

However, if **p_tm** is a pointer to a structure of type **date_time**, then the following statement is used.

    strcpy(tm − >date, "3/12/88");

THE COMMA OPERATOR

The comma operator is used mostly in the **for** statement. Its effect is to cause a sequence of operations to be performed. When it is used on the right side of an assignment statement, the value of the entire expression is the value of the last expression of the comma-separated list. For example:

    y = 10;
    x = (y = y − 5,25/y);

After execution, **x** will have the value 5 because **y**'s original value of 10 is reduced by 5, and then that value is divided into 25, yielding 5 as the result. You can think of the comma operator as meaning "do this and this."

SIZEOF

Although **sizeof** is also considered a keyword, it is a compile time operator used to determine the size, in bytes, of a variable or data type, including user-defined structures and unions. If it is used with a type, the type name must be enclosed by parentheses.

For most microcomputer-based C compilers, this example prints the number 2.

    int x;
    printf("%d", sizeof x);

THE CAST

A *cast* is a special operator that forces one data type to be converted into another. The general form is:

    (type) variable

For example, for the integer **count** to be used in a call
to **sqrt()**, C's standard library square-root routine that
requires a floating point parameter, a cast is used to force
count to be treated as type **float**, in this instance.

```
float y;
int count;
count = 10;
y = sqrt((float)count);
```

OPERATOR PRECEDENCE SUMMARY

The table below lists the precedence of all C operators.
Please note that all operators, except for the unary operators and ?, associate from left to right. The unary operators, * & -, and the ? operator associate from right to left.

highest	() [] -> .
	! ~ ++ -- - (type) * & sizeof
	* / %
	+ -
	<< >>
	< <= > >=
	== !=
	&
	^
	&&
	?:
	= += -= *= /= %= >>=
	<<= &= ^= |=
lowest	,

KEYWORD SUMMARY

As defined by the proposed ANSI standard, these are the 32 keywords that, combined with the formal C syntax, form the C language.

auto	double	int	struct
break	else	long	switch
case	enum	register	typedef
char	extern	return	union
const	float	short	unsigned
continue	for	signed	void
default	goto	sizeof	volatile
do	if	static	while

In addition to these keywords, many C compilers designed for use in a PC environment, such as Turbo C, have added the following keywords to allow greater control over the use of memory and other system resources.

_cs	_ds	_es	_ss
cdecl	far	huge	interrupt
near	pascal		

All C keywords are lowercase. In C, uppercase and lowercase are different; that is, **else** is a keyword, ELSE is not. Here follows a brief synopsis of the C keywords.

auto: **auto** is used to create temporary variables that are created upon entry into a block and are destroyed upon exit. Consider this program.

```
main()
{
    for(;;) {
        if(getche() = = 'a') {
            auto int t;
            for(t=0; t<'a'; t++)
                printf("%d ", t);
        }
    }
}
```

In this example, the variable **t** is created only if the user strikes an 'a'. Outside of the **if** block, **t** is completely unknown and any reference to it would generate a compile time syntax error.

break: **break** is used to exit from a **do**, **for**, or **while** loop, bypassing the normal loop condition. It is also used to exit from a **switch** statement.

An example of **break** in a loop follows.

```
while(x<100) {
    x = get_new_x();
    if(keystroke()) break; /* key hit on keyboard */
    process(x);
}
```

Here, if a key is typed, the loop will terminate no matter what the value of **x** is.

A **break** always terminates the innermost **for**, **do**, **while**, or **switch** statement, regardless of how these might be nested. In a **switch** statement, **break** effectively keeps program execution from "falling through" to the next **case**. (Refer to the **switch** statement for details.)

case: Refer to the **switch** statement.

cdecl: The **cdecl** keyword is not part of the ANSI standard. It forces a C compiler to compile a function so that its parameter passing conforms with the standard C calling convention. It is found in compilers that allow a Pascal calling convention to be specified. It is then used when you are compiling an entire file using the Pascal option and you want a specific function to be compatible with C.

char: **char** is a data type used to declare character variables.

const: The **const** modifier tells the compiler that the variable that follows may not be modified.

continue: **continue** is used to bypass portions of code in a loop and force the conditional test to be performed. For example, the following **while** loop will simply

read characters from the keyboard until an 's' is typed.
```
while(ch = getche()) {
    if(ch! = 's') continue; /* read another char */
    process(ch);
}
```
The call to **process()** will not occur until **ch** contains the character 's'.

default: **default** is used in the **switch** statement to signal a default block of code to be executed if no matches are found in the **switch**. See **switch**.

do: The **do** loop is one of three loop constructs available in C. The general form of the **do** loop is:
```
do {
    statement block
} while(condition);
```
If only one statement is repeated, the braces are not necessary. However, they do add clarity to the statement.

The **do** loop is the only loop in C that will always have at least one iteration because the condition is tested at the bottom of the loop.

A common use of the **do** loop is for reading disk files. The following fragment will read a file until an EOF is encountered.
```
do {
    ch = getc(fp);
    store(ch);
} while(!feof(fp));
```

double: **double** is a data type specifier used to declare double precision floating point variables.

else: See **if**.

enum: The **enum** type specifier is used to create enumeration types. An enumeration is simply a list of objects. Hence, an enumeration type specifies what that list of objects is. Further, an enumeration-type variable may only be assigned values that are part of the enumeration list. For example, the following code declares an enumeration called **color** and a variable of that type called **c** and performs an assignment and a condition test.

```
enum color {red, green, yellow ;
enum color c;
main()
{
    c = red;
    if(c = = red) printf("is red");
}
```

extern: **extern** is a data-type modifier used to tell the compiler that a variable is declared elsewhere in the program. This is often used in conjunction with separately compiled files that share the same global data and are linked together. In essence, it notifies the compiler of a variable without redeclaring it.

For example, if **first** were declared in another file as an integer, then in subsequent files the following declaration would be used:

```
extern int first;
```

far: The **far** type modifier is not part of the ANSI standard. It is used by compilers designed for use on the 8086 family of processors to force a pointer variable to use 32 rather than 16 bits.

float: **float** is a data type specifier used to declare floating point variables.

for: Allows automatic initialization and incrementation of a counter variable. The general form is:

```
for(initialization; condition; increment) {
    statement block
}
```

If the *statement block* is only one statement, then the braces are not necessary.

Although the **for** allows a number of variations, generally the *initialization* is used to set a counter variable to its starting value. The *condition* is generally a relational statement that checks the counter variable against a termination value, and *increment* increments (or decrements) the counter value.

The following code will print the message "hello" ten times.

```
for(t = 0; t<10; t + +) printf("hello/n");
```

goto: The **goto** causes program execution to "jump" to the label specified in the **goto** statement. The general form of the **goto** is:

```
    goto label;
    .
    .
    .
    label:
```

All labels must end in a colon and must not conflict with keywords or function names. Furthermore, a **goto** can only branch within the current function—not from one function to another.

The following example will print the message "right" but not the message "wrong".

```
    goto lab1;
        printf("wrong");
    lab1:
        printf("right");
```

huge: The **huge** type modifier is not part of the ANSI standard. It is used by compilers designed for use on the 8086 family of processors to force a pointer variable to use 32 bits rather than 16. It also lets the object pointed to be larger than one segment (64K).

if: The general form of the **if** statement is

```
    if(condition) {
        statement block 1
    }
    else {
        statement block 2
    }
```

29

If single statements are used, the braces are not needed. The **else** is optional.

The condition may be any expression. If that expression evaluates to any value other than 0, then *statement block 1* will be executed; otherwise, if it exists, *statement block 2* will be executed.

The following fragment checks for the letter 'q', which terminates the program.

```
ch = getche();
if(ch = = 'q') {
    printf("program terminated");
    exit(0);
}
else proceed();
```

int: **int** is the type specifier used to declare integer variables.

interrupt: The **interrupt** type specifier is specific to compilers designed for use on the 8086 family of processors and is not part of the ANSI standard. It is used to declare functions that will be used as interrupt service routines.

long: **long** is a data-type modifier that is used to declare double-length integer variables.

near: The **near** type modifier is not part of the ANSI standard. It is used by compilers designed for use on the 8086 family of processors to force a pointer variable to use 16 bits rather than 32.

pascal: The **pascal** keyword is not defined by the ANSI standard. It is used to force a C compiler to compile a function in such a way that its parameter passing convention is compatible with Pascal rather than with C.

register: **register** is a declaration modifier that is used to force either an integer or a character to be stored in a register of the CPU instead of being placed in memory. It can only be used on local variables.

return: The **return** statement forces a return from a function and can be used to transfer a value back to the calling routine.

For example, the following function returns the product of its two integer arguments.

```
mul(a, b)
int a, b;
{
    return(a*b);
}
```

Keep in mind that as soon as a **return** is encountered, the function will return, skipping any other code that may be in the function.

sizeof: The **sizeof** compile time operator returns the length of the variable it precedes. For example:

```
printf("%d", sizeof(int));
```

will print a 2 for most microcomputer-based C compilers.

sizeof's principal use is to help generate portable code when that code depends upon the size of the C built-in data types.

signed: The **signed** type modifier is used to specify a **signed char** data type.

short: **short** is a data-type modifier that is used to declare integers that are one byte long.

static: **static** is a data-type modifier that is used to instruct the compiler to create permanent storage for the local variable that it precedes. This enables the specified variable to maintain its value between function calls.

struct: The **struct** keyword is used to create complex or conglomerate variables, called structures, that are made up of one or more elements of the seven basic data types. The general form of a structure is:

```
struct struct_name {
    type element1;
    type element2;
        .
        .
        .
    type elementn;
} structure_variable_name;
```

The individual elements are referenced by using the dot or arrow operators.

switch: The **switch** statement is C's multi-way branch statement. It is used to route execution one of several different ways. The general form of the statement is:

```
switch(control_var) {
    case (constant1): statement sequence 1;
        break;
    case (constant2): statement sequence 2;
        break;
        .
        .
        .
    case (constant n): statement sequence n;
        break;
    default: default statements;
}
```

Each *statement sequence* may be from one to several statements long. The **default** portion is optional.

The **switch** works by checking *control_var* against the constants. If a match is found, that sequence of statements is executed. If the **break** statement is omitted, execution will continue until the end of the **switch**. You can think of the **case**s as labels. Execution will continue until a **break** statement is found, or the **switch** ends. If no match is found and a **default** case exists, its statement sequence is executed. Otherwise, no action takes place.

The following example processes a menu selection.

```
ch = getche();
switch (ch) {
    case 'e': enter();
        break;
    case 'l': list();
        break;
    case 's': sort();
        break;
    case 'q': exit(0);
    default: printf("unknown command");
        printf("try again");
}
```

typedef: The **typedef** keyword allows you to create a new name for an existing data type. The data type may be either one of the built-in types, or a structure or union name. The general form of **typedef** is:

    typedef type_specifier new_name;

For example, to use the word **balance** in place of **float**, you would write:

    typedef float balance;

union: **union** is used to assign two or more variables to the same memory location. The form of the definition and the way the **.** (dot) and -> (arrow) operators reference an element are the same as for **struct**. The general form is:

    union union_name {
        type element1;
        type element2;
        .
        .
        .
        type elementN;
    } union variable_name;

unsigned: **unsigned** is a data-type modifier that tells the compiler to eliminate the sign bit of an integer and to use all bits for arithmetic. This has the effect of doubling the size of the largest integer, but restricts it to only positive numbers.

void: The **void** type specifier is primarily used to explicitly declare functions that return no (meaningful) value. It is also used to create **void** pointers (pointers to **void**), which are generic pointers capable of pointing to any type of object.

volatile: The **volatile** modifier is used to tell the compiler that a variable may have its contents altered in ways not explicitly defined by the program. For example, variables that are changed by hardware such as real-time clocks, interrupts, or other inputs should be declared as **volatile**.

while: The **while** loop has the general form

```
while(condition) {
    statement block
}
```

If a single statement is the object of the **while**, then the braces may be omitted.

The **while** tests its *condition* at the top of the loop. Therefore, if the *condition* is FALSE to begin with, the loop will not execute at all. The *condition* may be any expression.

An example of a **while** follows. It will read 100 characters from a disk file and store them into a character array.

```
t = 0;
while(t<100) {
    s[t] = getc(fp);
    t++;
}
```

_cs, _ds, _es, _ss: The **_cs, _ds, _es, _ss** modifiers tell the C compiler which segment register to use when evaluating a pointer. For example, this instructs the compiler to use the extra segment when using **ptr**.

```
int _es *ptr;
```

Frankly, there will be few, if any, times when you will need to use these segment register overrides.

THE C PREPROCESSOR

C includes several preprocessor commands that are used to give instructions to the compiler.

#define

#define is used to perform macro-substitutions of one piece of text for another throughout the file in which it is used. The general form of the directive is:

    ##define name string

Notice that there is no semicolon in this statement.

For example, if you wish to use the word TRUE for the value 1 and the word FALSE for the value 0, then you would declare two macro **#defines:**

    #define TRUE 1
    #define FALSE 0

This will cause the compiler to substitute a 1 or a 0 each time the name TRUE or FALSE is encountered.

#error

The **#error** directive forces the compiler to stop compilation when it is encountered. It is used primarily for debugging. Its general form is:

    #error message

When **#error** is encountered, the message and the line number are displayed.

#include

The **#include** preproccessor directive instructs the compiler to read and compile another source file. The source file to be read in must be enclosed between double quotes or angle brackets. If quotes are used, the current working directory is searched first for the file. If it is not found, the standard include directory is searched. If angle brackets are used, the current working directory is not searched—only the standard include directory is. For example:

```
#include "stdio.h"
```

will instruct the C compiler to read and compile the header for the disk file library routines.

#if, #ifdef, #ifndef, #else, #elif, #endif

These preprocessor directives are used to selectively compile various portions of a program. The general idea is that if the expression after a **#if, #ifdef** or **#ifndef** is TRUE, then the code that is between one of the preceding and an **#endif** will be compiled; otherwise it will be skipped over. **#endif** is used to mark the end of a **#if** block. The **#else** can be used with any of the above similar to the **else** in the C **if** statement. The general form of **#if** is:

```
#if constant expression
```

If the constant expression is TRUE, then the block of code will be compiled.

The general form of **#ifdef** is

```
#ifdef name
```

If the **name** has been defined in a **#define** statement, the following block of code will be compiled.

The general form of **#ifndef** is

```
#ifndef name
```

If **name** is currently undefined, then the block of code is compiled.

For example, here is how some of the these preprocessor directives work together.

```
#define ted 10
main()
{
#ifdef ted
    printf("Hi Ted/n");
```

```
#endif
    printf("bye bye/n");
#if 10<9
    printf("Hi George/n");
#endif
}
```
will print "Hi Ted" and "bye bye" one the screen, but not "Hi George".

The **#elif** directive is used to create an if-else-if statement. Its general form is:

    #elif constant-expression

The **#elif** may be used with the **#if** but not the **#ifdef** or **#ifndef** directives.

I/O FUNCTIONS

The functions that comprise the C input/output system can be grouped into three major catagories: console I/O, buffered file I/O, and the UNIX-like unbuffered file I/O. Strictly speaking, console I/O is made up of functions that are special case versions of the more general functions found in the buffered file system. It is sometimes easier for beginners to think of the console I/O routines as separate from the file routines. However, remember that a common interface is used for the console and file I/O functions. The unbuffered UNIX-like I/O system is not defined by the proposed ANSI standard and is expected to decline in popularity. The UNIX-like I/O system functions are included in this chapter because they are still widely used in existing programs. The UNIX-like file system and the buffered file system are completely separate.

The operation of the UNIX-like routines is self-evident from their descriptions. However, to understand the operation of the ANSI standard buffered file system, you must understand streams.

Streams: The buffered file system is designed to work with a wide variety of devices, including terminals, disk drives, and tape drives. Even though each device is very different, the buffered file system transforms each into a logical device called a *stream*. All streams are similar in their behavior. Because streams are largely device independent, the same functions that write to a disk file can also write to the console. There are two types of streams: text and binary.

A *text stream* is a sequence of characters organized into lines terminated by a newline character. The proposed ANSI standard states that the newline character is optional, depending upon the implementation. In a text stream, certain character translations may occur as required by the host environment. For example, a newline may be converted to a carriage return, line-feed pair. Therefore, there may not be a one-to-one relationship between the characters that are written (read) and those in the external device. Also, because of possible translations, the number of characters written (read) may not be the same as those found in the external device.

A *binary stream* is a sequence of bytes that have a one-to-one correspondence to those found in the external device. That is, no character translations will occur. Also, the number of bytes written (read) will be the same as those found in the external device. The proposed standard does specify, however, that a binary stream may have an implementation-defined number of null bytes appended to its end. These null bytes might be used to pad the information so that it fills a sector on a disk, for example.

Files: In C, a *file* is a logical concept that may be applied to everything from disk files to terminals. A stream is associated with a specific file by performing an open operation. Once a file is open, then information may be exchanged between it and your program.

Not all files have the same capabilities. For example, a disk file can support random access, while a terminal cannot. This illustrates an important point about the C I/O system: All streams are the same, but all files are not.

If the file can support random access (sometimes referred to as *position requests*), then opening that file also initializes the *file position indicator* to the start of the file. As each character is read from or written to the file, the position indicator is incremented, thus ensuring progression through the file.

A stream is disassociated from a specific file through a close operation. On files opened for output, closing a file causes the contents, if any, of its associated stream to be written to the external device. This process is generally referred to as *flushing* the file and it guarantees that no information is accidentally left in the disk buffer. The proposed ANSI standard states that whether a zero-length file will actually exist after it is closed is implementation dependent. All files are closed automatically when your program terminates normally by **main()** returning to the operating system or by a call to **exit().** Files are not closed when a program terminates through a call to **abort()** or, obviously, if it crashes.

At the beginning of a program's execution, three predefined text streams are opened. They are **stdin**, **stdout**, and **stderr** and they refer to the standard I/O device connected to the system. For most systems this is the console. Remember, however, that most operating systems allow I/O redirection, so routines that read or write to these files may be redirected to other devices. (Redirection of I/O is the process whereby information that would normally go to one device is rerouted to another device by the operating system.) You should never try to explicitly open or close these files.

Each stream that is associated with a file has a file-control structure of type **FILE**. This structure is defined in the header **stdio.h.** No programmer modifications to, or manipulations of, this file control block should ever be undertaken.

Conceptual vs. Actual: In light of the foregoing discussion, the following summarizes the way the C I/O system operates. As far as the programmer is concerned, all I/O takes place through *streams,* which are sequences of characters. Further, all streams are the same. The file system links a stream to a *file*. In the language of C programmers, a file is any external device capabile of I/O. Because different devices have differing capabilities, all files are not the same. However, these differences, as they relate to the programmer, are minimized by the C I/O system because this system converts the raw information coming from the device into a stream (and vice versa). Aside from the limitation that only certain types of files support random access, the programmer need not worry about the actual physical device and is free to concentrate on the logical device.

Note: Functions declared as returning **void** are so displayed. In a nonstandard implementation, most of these functions will be defaulted to **int**.

► **#include "stdio.h"**
void clearerr(stream)
FILE *stream;

The **clearerr()** function is used to reset the file error flag pointed to by *stream* to zero (off). The end-of-file indicator is also reset.

The error flags for each stream are initially set to zero by a successful call to **fopen()**. Once an error has occurred, the flags stay set until either an explicit call to **clearerr()** or **rewind()** is made.

File errors can occur for a wide variety of reasons, many of which are system dependent. The exact nature of the error can be determined by calling **perror()**, which displays what error has occurred (see **perror()**).

Related functions: **feof()**, **ferror()**, and **perror()**

► **#include "stdio.h"**
int close(fd)
int fd;

The **close()** function belongs to the UNIX-like file system and is not defined by the proposed ANSI standard. When **close()** is called with a valid file descriptor, it closes the file associated with it and flushes the write-buffers, if applicable. (File descriptors are created through a successful call to **open()** or **creat()** and do not relate to streams or file pointers.)

When successful, **close()** returns a 0; otherwise −1 is returned. Although there are several reasons why a file may not be able to be closed, the most common is the premature removal of the medium. For example, if a diskette is removed from the drive before the file is closed, an error will result.

In some C implementations, especially those that support the proposed ANSI standard, the header information necessary to the UNIX-like file system is no longer kept in **stdio.h** but rather in its own separate file. Check your user manual.

Related functions: **open()**, **creat()**, **read()**, **write()**, **unlink()**

```
#include "stdio.h"
```
▶ **int creat(filename,pmode)**
```
char *filename;
int pmode;
```

The **creat()** function is part of the UNIX-like file system and is not defined by the proposed ANSI standard. Its purpose is to create a new file with the name pointed to by **filename** and to open it for writing. On success, **creat()** returns a file descriptor that is greater than or equal to 0; on failure, −1 is returned. (File descriptors are integers and do not relate to streams or file pointers.)

The value of *pmode* determines the file's access setting, sometimes called its *permission mode*. The value of *pmode* is highly dependent upon the operating system; you must check the user manual for exact details. In general, the access modes a file may have include read-only, read/write, and a security access setting.

If, at the time of the call to **creat()**, the specified file is already existent, it will be erased and all previous contents will be lost.

In some C implementations, especially those that support the proposed ANSI standard, the header information necessary to the UNIX-like file system is no longer kept in **stdio.h** but rather in its own separate file. You should check your user manual.

Related functions: **open()**, **close()**, **read()**, **write()**, **unlink()**, **eof()**

▶ ```
#include "stdio.h"
int eof(fd)
int fd;
```

The **eof()** function is part of the UNIX-like file system and is not defined by the proposed ANSI standard. When called with a valid file descriptor, **eof()** returns 1 if the end of the file has been reached; otherwise a 0 is returned. If an error has occurred, $a - 1$ is returned. In some C implementations, especially those that support the proposed ANSI standard, the header information necessary to the UNIX-like file system is no longer kept in **stdio.h** but rather in its own separate file. Check your user manual.

Related functions: **open()**, **close()**, **read()**, **write()**, **unlink()**

▶ ```
#include "stdio.h"
int fclose(stream)
FILE *stream;
```

The **fclose()** function closes the file associated with *stream* and flushes its buffer. After an **fclose()**, *stream* is no longer connected with the file and any automatically allocated buffers are deallocated.

If **fclose()** is successful, a 0 is returned; otherwise a non-zero number is returned. Trying to close a file that has already been closed is an error.

Related functions: **fopen()**, **freopen()**, **fflush()**

#include "stdio.h"
▶ int feof(stream)
FILE *stream;

The **feof()** checks the file position indicator to determine if the end of the file associated with *stream* has been reached. A non-zero value is returned if the file position indicator is at end-of-file; a 0 is returned otherwise.

Once the end of the file has been reached, subsequent read operations will return **EOF** until either **rewind()** is called or the file position indicator is moved, using **fseek()**.

The **feof()** function is particularly useful when working with binary files, because the end-of-file marker is also a valid binary integer. Explicit calls must be made to **feof()** rather than simply testing the return value of **getc()**, for example, to determine when the end of the file has been reached.

Related functions: **clearerr()**, **ferror()**, **perror()**, **putc()**, **getc()**

#include "stdio.h"
▶ int ferror(stream)
FILE *stream;

The **ferror()** function checks for a file error on the given *stream*. A return value of 0 indicates that no error has occurred, while a non-zero value means an error. The error flags associated with stream will stay set until either the file is closed, or **rewind()** or **clearerr()** is called. To determine the exact nature of the error, use the **perror()** function.

Related functions: **clearerr()**, **feof()**, **perror()**

#include "stdio.h"
▶ **int fflush(stream);**
   FILE *stream;

If *stream* is associated with a file opened for writing, a call to **fflush()** causes the contents of the output buffer to be physically written to the file. If *stream* points to an input file, then the contents of the input buffer are cleared. In either case the file remains open. A return value of 0 indicates success, while non-zero means that a write error has occurred.

All buffers are automatically flushed upon normal termination of the program or when they are full. Also, closing a file flushes its buffer.

Related functions: **fclose()**, **fopen()**, **fread()**, **fwrite()**, **getc()**, **putc()**

#include "stdio.h"
▶ **int fgetc(stream);**
   FILE *stream;

The **fgetc()** function returns the next character from the input *stream* from the current position and increments the file position indicator. The character is read as an *unsigned char* that is converted to an integer.

If the end of the file is reached, **fgetc()** returns **EOF**. However, since **EOF** is a valid integer value, when working with binary files you must use **feof()** to check for end-of-file. If **fgetc()** encounters an error, **EOF** is also returned. Again, when working with binary files you must use **ferror()** to check for file errors.

Related functions: **fputc()**, **getc()**, **putc()**, **fopen()**

```
#include "stdio.h"
```
▶ char *fgets(str,num,stream)
```
char *str;
int num;
FILE *stream;
```

The **fgets()** function reads up to **num-1** characters from *stream* and places them into the character array pointed to by *str*. Characters are read until either a newline or an EOF is received, or until the specified limit is reached. After the characters have been read, a null is placed in the array immediately after the last character read. A newline character will be retained and will be part of *str*.

If successful, **fgets()** returns *str*; a null pointer is returned upon failure. If a read error occurs, the contents of the array pointed to by *str* are indeterminate. Because a null pointer will be returned either when an error has occurred or when the end of the file is reached, use **feof()** or **ferror()** to determine what has actually happened.

Related functions: **fputs()**, **fgetc()**, **gets()**, **puts()**

```
#include "stdio.h"
```
▶ FILE *fopen(fname,mode)
```
char *fname;
char *mode;
```

The **fopen()** function opens a file whose name is pointed to by *fname* and returns the stream that is associated with it. The type of operations that will be allowed on the file are defined by the value of *mode*. The legal values for *mode* as proposed by the ANSI standard are shown below. (Note that the traditional values for *mode* are "r" for read, "w" for write, and "rw" for read/write. Many implementations still use this approach.) The filename must be a string of characters that comprise a valid filename as defined by the operating system, and may include a path specification if the environment supports it.

If **fopen()** is successful in opening the specified file, then a **FILE** pointer is returned. If the file cannot be opened, a null pointer is returned.

The legal values for mode

Mode	Meaning
"r"	open text file for reading
"w"	create a text file for writing
"a"	append to text file
"rb"	open binary file for reading
"wb"	create binary file for writing
"ab"	append to a binary file
"r+"	open text file for read/write
"w+"	create text file for read/write
"a+"	open text file for read/write
"rb+"	open binary file for read/write
"wb+"	create binary file for read/write
"ab+"	open binary file for read/write

As the table shows, a file may be opened in either text or binary mode. In text mode, carriage-return/linefeed sequences are translated to newline characters on input. On output, the reverse occurs: newlines are translated to carriage-return/linefeeds. No such translations occur on binary files.

If you use **fopen()** to open a file for write, then any pre-existing file by that name will be erased and a new file will be started. If no file by that name exists, then one will be created. If you want to add to the end of the file, then you must use mode "a". If the file does not exist, an error will be returned. Opening a file for read operations requires that the file exists. If it does not, an error will be returned. Finally, if a file is opened for read/write operations it will not be erased if it exists; however, if it does not exist it will be created.

Related functions: **fclose()**, **fread()**, **fwrite()**, **putc()**, **getc()**

#include "stdio.h"

▶ int fprintf(stream, format, arg-list)
FILE *stream;
char *format;

The **fprintf()** function outputs the values of the arguments that comprise *arg-list,* as specified in the *format* string to the stream pointed to by *stream.* The return value is the number of characters actually printed. If an error occurs, a negative number is returned.

There may be from zero to several arguments. The maximum number will be system dependent. The operations of the format control string and commands are identical to those in **printf()**; see the **printf()** function for a complete description.

Related functions: **printf()**, **fscanf()**

#include "stdio.h"

▶ int fputc(ch, stream)
int ch;
FILE *stream;

The **fputc()** function writes the character *ch* to the specified stream at current file position and then advances the file position indicator. Even though *ch* is declared to be an **int** for historical purposes, it is converted by **fputc()** into an **unsigned char**. Because all character arguments are elevated to integers at the time of the call, you will generally see character variables used as arguments. If an integer were used, the high order byte would simply be discarded.

The value returned by **fputc()** is the value of the character written. If an error occurs, **EOF** is returned. For files opened for binary operations, a **EOF** may be a valid character and the function **ferror()** will need to be used to determine whether an error has actually occurred.

Related functions: **fgetc()**, **fopen()**, **fprintf()**, **fread()**, **fwrite()**

#include "stdio.h"
▶ **int fputchar(ch)**
int ch;

The **fputchar()** function writes the character *ch* to **stdout**. Even though *ch* is declared to be an **int** for historical purposes, it is converted by **fputchar()** into an **unsigned char**. Because all character arguments are elevated to integers at the time of the call, you will generally see character variables used as arguments. If an integer were used, the high-order byte would simply be discarded. A call to **fputchar()** is the functional equivalent of a call to **fputc(ch, stdout)**.

The value returned by **fputchar()** is the value of the character written. If an error occurs, **EOF** is returned. For files opened for binary operations, an **EOF** may be a valid character and the function **ferror()** will need to be used to determine whether an error has actually occurred.

Related functions: **fgetc()**, **fopen()**, **fprintf()**, **fread()**, **fwrite()**

#include "stdio.h"
▶ **int fputs(str, stream)**
char *str;
FILE *stream;

The **fputs()** function writes the contents of the string pointed to by **str** to the specified stream. The null terminator is not written. The **fputs()** function returns 0 on success, non-zero on failure.

If the stream is opened in text mode, certain character translations may take place. This means that there may not be a one-to-one mapping of the string onto the file. However, if opened in binary mode, no character translations will occur and a one-to-one mapping between the string and the file will exist.

Related functions: **fgets()**, **gets()**, **puts()**, **fprintf()**, **fscanf()**

```
#include "stdio.h"
```
▶ **int fread(buf, size, count, stream)**
```
void *buf; /* implementations lacking void
              use char */
int size, count;
FILE *stream;
```

The **fread()** function reads *count* number of objects, each object being *size* number of characters in length, from the stream pointed to by *stream* and places them in the character array pointed to by *buf.* The file position indicator is advanced by the number of characters read.

The **fread()** function returns the number of characters actually read. If fewer characters are read than are requested in the call, either an error has occurred or the end of the file has been reached. You must use **feof()** or **ferror()** to determine what has taken place.

If the stream is opened for text operations, then carriage-return/linefeed sequences are automatically translated into newlines.

Related functions: **fwrite()**, **fopen()**, **fscanf()**, **fgetc()**, **getc()**

```
#include "stdio.h"
```
▶ **FILE *freopen(fname, mode, stream)**
```
char *fname;
char *mode;
FILE *stream;
```

The **freopen()** function is used to associate an existing stream with a different file. The new file's name is pointed to by *fname*, the access mode is pointed to by *mode*, and the stream to be reassigned is pointed to by *stream*. The string *mode* uses the same format as **fopen()**; a complete discussion is found in the **fopen()** description.

When called, **freopen()** first tries to close a file that may currently be associated with *stream*. However, failure to achieve a successful closing is ignored and the attempt to reopen continues.

The **freopen**() function returns a pointer to *stream* on success and a null pointer otherwise.

The main use of **freopen**() is to redirect the system-defined files **stdin**, **stdout**, and **stderr** to some other file.

Related functions: **fopen**(), **fclose**()

▶ #include "stdio.h"
int fscanf(stream, format, arg-list)
FILE *stream;
char *format;

The **fscanf**() function works exactly like the **scanf**() function except that it reads the information from the stream specified by *stream* instead of **stdin**. See the **scanf**() function for details.

The **fscanf**() function returns the number of arguments actually assigned values. This number does not include skipped fields. A return value of **EOF** means that an attempt was made to read past the end of the file.

Related functions: **scanf**(), **fprintf**()

▶ #include "stdio.h"
int fseek(stream, offset, origin)
FILE *stream;
long offset;
int origin;

The **fseek**() function sets the file position indicator associated with *stream* according to the values of *offset* and *origin*. Its main purpose is to support random I/O operations. The *offset* is the number of bytes from origin to make the new position. The *origin* is either a 0, 1, or 2, with 0 being the start of the file, 1 the current position, and 2 the end of the file. The proposed ANSI standard specifies the following names for *origin*.

Origin	Name
beginning of file	SEEK_SET
current position	SEEK_CUR
end of file	SEEK_END

A return value of 0 means that **fseek()** succeeded. A non-zero value indicates failure.

In most implementations, and specified by the proposed ANSI standard, *offset* must be a **long int**. This is required to support files larger than 64K bytes.

If **fseek()** is implemented according to the proposed ANSI standard, then its use on text files is not recommended because the character translations will cause position errors to result. Therefore, its use is suggested only for binary files.

You may use **fseek()** to move the position indicator anywhere in the file, even beyond the end. However, it is an error to attempt to set the position indicator before the beginning of the file.

The **fseek()** function clears the end-of-file flag associated with the specified stream. Furthermore, it nullifies any prior **ungetc()** on the same stream. (See **ungetc()**).

Related functions: **ftell()**, **rewind()**, **fopen()**

#include "stdio.h"
▶ **long ftell(stream)**
  FILE *stream;

The **ftell()** function returns the current value of the file position indicator for the specified stream. In the case of binary streams, the value is the number of bytes the indicator is from the beginning of the file. For text streams the return value is undefined because of possible character translations, such as carriage-return/linefeeds being substituted for newlines. However, when applied to text streams, this value returned may be used as an argument to **fseek()** to return to a previous position.

The **ftell()** function returns − 1L when an error occurs. If the stream is incapable of random seeks—if it is a terminal, for instance—then the return value is undefined.

Related function: **fseek()**

#include "stdio.h"
▶ **int fwrite(buf, size, count, stream)**
**void *buf; /* implementations lacking void use
char */**
int size, count;
FILE *stream;

The **fwrite()** function writes *count* number of objects, each object being *size* number of characters in length, to the stream pointed to by stream from the character array pointed to by *buf*. The file position indicator is advanced by the number of characters written.

The **fwrite()** function returns the number of characters actually written. If the function is successful, this number will equal the number requested. If fewer characters are written than are requested, this implies that an error has occurred. For text streams, various character translations may take place but will have no effect upon the return value.

Related functions: **fread()**, **fscanf()**, **getc()**, **fgetc()**

#include "stdio.h"
▶ **int getc(stream)**
FILE *stream;

The **getc()** function returns the next character from the input *stream* from the current position and increments the file position indicator. The character is read as an **unsigned char** that is converted to an integer.

If the end of the file is reached, **getc()** returns **EOF**. However, since **EOF** is a valid integer value, when working with binary files you must use **feof()** to check for end-of-file. If **getc()** encounters an error, **EOF** is also returned. Again, when working with binary files you must use **ferror()** to check for file errors.

Related functions: **fputc()**, **fgetc()**, **putc()**, **fopen()**

```
#include "stdio.h"
```
▶ **int getchar()**

The **getchar()** function returns the next character from **stdin.** The character is read as an **unsigned char** that is converted to an integer.

If the end of the file is reached, **getc()** returns **EOF**. However, since **EOF** is a valid integer value, when working with binary files you must use **feof()** to check for end-of-file. If **getc()** encounters an error, **EOF** is also returned. Again, when working with binary files you must use **ferror()** to check for file errors.

The functions **getchar()** and **fgetchar()** are identical, and in most implementations **getchar()** is simply defined as a macro. This causes the **fgetchar()** function to be substituted for the **getchar()** macro.

The **getchar()** function (or macro) is functionally equivalent to **getc(stdin).**

Related functions: **fputc()**, **fgetc()**, **putc()**, **fopen()**

```
#include "stdio.h"
```
▶ **char *gets(str)**
  char *str;

The **gets()** function reads characters from **stdin** and places them into the character array pointed to by *str*. Characters are read until a newline or an **EOF** is received. The newline character is not made part of the string; instead it is translated into a null to terminate the string.

If successful, **gets()** returns *str*; a null pointer is returned upon failure. If a read error occurs, the contents of the array pointed to by **str** are indeterminate. Because a null pointer will be returned when either an error has occurred or when the end of the file is reached, use **feof()** or **ferror()** to determine what has actually happened.

There is no limit to the number of characters that **gets()** will read and it is therefore your job to make sure that the array pointed to by *str* will not be overrun.

Related functions: **fputs()**, **fgetc()**, **fgets()**, **puts()**

#include "stdio.h"
▶ int getw(stream)
FILE *stream;

The **getw()** function is not defined by the proposed ANSI standard, and its use may cause portability problems. The **getw()** function returns the next integer from *stream* and advances the file-position indicator appropriately.

Because the integer read may have a value equal to **EOF**, use **feof()** and/or **ferror()** to determine when end-of-file is reached or whether an error has occurred.

Related functions: **putw()**, **fread()**

▶ int kbhit()

The **kbhit()** function is not defined by the proposed ANSI standard. However, it is found, under various names, in virtually all C implementations. It returns a non-zero value if a key has been pressed at the console, and returns 0 otherwise. Its main use is to allow a routine to be interrupted by the user. It may require a header file for use in certain implementations.

Related functions: **fgetc()**, **getc()**

#include "stdio.h"
▶ long lseek(fd, offset, origin)
int fd;
long offset;
int origin;

The **lseek()** function is part of the UNIX-like I/O system and is not defined by the proposed ANSI standard.

The **lseek()** function sets the file position indicator to the location specified by *offset* and *origin* for the file specified by *fd*.

How **lseek()** works depends on the values of *origin* and *offset*. The *origin* may be either a 0, 1, or 2. The chart shown here explains how the *offset* is interpreted for each *origin* value.

Origin	Effect of Call to lseek()
0	count the offset from the start of the file
1	count the offset from the current position
2	count the offset from the end of the file

The **lseek()** function returns *offset* on success. Therefore, **lseek()** will be returning a **long** integer and must be declared as such at the top of your program. Upon failure, a − 1L is returned.

In some C implementations, especially those that support the proposed ANSI standard, the header information necessary to the UNIX-like file system is no longer kept in **stdio.h** but rather in its own separate file. Check your user manual.

Related functions: **read()**, **write()**, **open()**, **close()**

```
#include "stdio.h"
```
▶ **int open(fname, mode)**
```
char *fname;
int mode;
```

The **open()** function is part of the UNIX-like I/O system and is not defined by the proposed ANSI standard.

Unlike the buffered I/O system, the UNIX-like system does not use file pointers of type FILE, but rather file descriptors of type **int**. The **open()** function opens a file with the name *fname* and sets its access mode as specified by *mode*. The values that *mode* may have are:

Mode	Effect
0	read
1	write
2	read/write

Note: many compilers have additional modes, such as text, binary, and the like, so check your user manual. Also, many compilers have defined macros, such as **O_RDONLY** to open for read operations, that can be used in place of the integer values just given.

A successful call to **open()** returns a positive integer that is the file descriptor associated with the file. A return value of −1 means that the file cannot be opened.

In most implementations, if the file specified in the **open()** statement does not appear on the disk, the operation will fail—the file will not be created. However, depending upon the implementation, you may be able to use **open()** to create a file that is currently nonexistent. Check your user manual.

In some C implementations, especially those that support the proposed ANSI standard, the header information necessary to the UNIX-like file system is no longer kept in **stdio.h** but rather in its own separate file. Check your user manual.

Related functions: **close()**, **read()**, **write()**

#include "stdio.h"
▶ **int printf(format, arg-list)**
   char *format;

The **printf()** function writes to **stdout** the arguments that comprise *arg-list* under the control of the string pointed to by *format*.

The string pointed to by *format* consists of two types of items. The first type is made up of characters that will be printed on the screen. The second type contains format commands that define the way the arguments are displayed. A format command begins with a percent sign and is followed by the format code. The format commands are shown below. There must be exactly the same number of arguments as there are format commands, and the format commands and the arguments are matched in order. For example, this **printf()** call

```
printf("Hi %c %d %s",'c',10,"there!");
```

displays: "Hi c 10 there!".

If there are insufficient arguments to match the format commands, the output is undefined. If there are more arguments than format commands, the remaining arguments are discarded.

Code	Format
%c	a single character
%d	decimal
%i	decimal
%e	scientific notation
%f	decimal floating point
%g	uses %e or %f, whichever is shorter
%o	octal
%s	string of characters
%u	unsigned decimal
%x	hexadecimal
%%	prints a % sign
%p	displays a pointer
%n	the associated argument shall be an integer pointer into which is placed the number of characters written so far

The **printf()** function returns the number of characters actually printed. A negative return value indicates that an error has taken place.

The format commands may have modifiers that specify the field width, the number of decimal places, and a left-justification flag. An integer placed between the % sign and the format command acts as a *minimum field width specifier.* This pads the output with blanks or zeros to ensure that it is at least a certain minimum length. If the string or number is greater than that minimum, it will be printed in full even if it overruns the minimum. The default padding is done with spaces. If you wish to pad with 0s, place a 0 before the field-width specifier. For example, %05d will pad a number of fewer than five digits with zeroes so that its total length is 5.

To specify the number of decimal places printed for a floating point number, place a decimal point followed by the number of decimal places you wish to display after the field-width specifier. For example, %10.4f will display a number at least ten characters wide with four decimal places. When this is applied to strings or integers, the number following the period specifies the maximum field length. For example, %5.7s will display a string that will be at least five characters long and will not exceed seven. If the string is longer than the maximum field width, the characters will be truncated off the end.

By default, all output is *right-justified*: if the field width is larger than the data printed, the data will be placed on the right edge of the field. You can force the information to be left-justified by placing a minus sign directly after the %. For example, %-10.2f will left-justify a floating point number with two decimal places in a ten-character field.

There are two format command modifiers that allow **printf()** to display **short** and **long** integers. These modifiers may be applied to the **d, i, o, u,** and **x** type specifiers. The **l** modifier tells **printf()** that a **long** data type follows. For example, **%ld** means that a **long int** is to be displayed. The **h** modifier instructs **printf()** to display a **short int.** Therefore, **%hu** indicates that the data is of type **short unsigned int.**

The **l** modifier may also prefix the floating point commands of **e, f,** and **g** and indicates that a **double** follows.
The **%n** command causes the number of characters that have been written at the time the **%n** is encountered to be placed in an integer variable whose pointer is specified in the argument list.

Related functions: **scanf(), fprintf()**

```
#include "stdio.h"
```
▶ **int putc(ch, stream)**
```
int ch;
FILE *stream;
```

The **putc()** function writes the character contained in the least significant byte of *ch* to the output stream pointed to by *stream*. Because character arguments are elevated to integer at the time of the call, you may use character variables as arguments to **putc()**.

The **putc()** function returns the character written on success or **EOF** if an error occurs. If the output stream has been opened in binary mode, then **EOF** is a valid value for *ch*. This means that you must use **ferror()** to determine if an error has occurred.

The **putc()** function is often implemented as a macro, substituting **fputc()** because **fputc()** is functionally equivalent to **putc()**.

Related functions: **fgetc()**, **fputc()**, **getchar()**, **putchar()**

```
#include "stdio.h"
```
▶ **int putchar(ch)**
```
int ch;
```

The **putchar()** function writes the character contained in the least significant byte of *ch* to **stdout**. It is functionally equivalent to **putc(ch,stdout)**. Because character arguments are elevated to integer at the time of the call, you may use character variables as arguments to **putchar()**.

The **putchar()** function returns the character written on success or **EOF** if an error occurs. If the output stream has been opened in binary mode then **EOF** is a valid value for *ch*. This means that you must use **ferror()** to determine if an error has occurred.

The **putchar()** function is often implemented as a macro, substituting **fputchar()** because **fputchar()** is functionally equivalent to **putchar()**.

Related functions: **fputchar()**, **putc()**

```
#include "stdio.h"
```
► **int puts(str)**
   char *str;

The **puts()** function writes the string pointed to by *str* to the standard output device. The null terminator is translated to a newline.

The **puts()** function returns a newline if successful, and an **EOF** if a failure.

Related functions: **putc()**, **gets()**, **printf()**

```
#include "stdio.h"
```
► **int putw(i, stream)**
   int i;
   FILE *stream;

The **putw()** function is not defined by the proposed ANSI standard and may not be fully portable. The **putw()** function writes the integer *i* to *stream* at the current file position and increments the file position pointer appropriately.

The **putw()** function returns the value written. A return value of **EOF** means an error has occurred in the stream if it is in text mode. Because **EOF** is also a valid integer value, you must use **ferror()** to detect an error in a binary stream.

Related functions: **getw()**, **printf()**, **fwrite()**

```
#include "stdio.h"
```
► **int read(fd, buf, count)**
   int fd;
   char *buf;
   unsigned int count;

The **read()** function is part of the UNIX-like I/O system and is not defined by the proposed ANSI standard.

The **read()** function reads *count* number of bytes from the file described by *fd* into the buffer pointed to by *buf*.

The file position indicator is adjusted forward by the number of bytes read. If the file is opened in text mode then character translations may take place.

The return value will be equal to the number of bytes actually read. This number may be smaller than *count* if either an end-of-file or an error is encountered. A value of −1 means an error, and a value of 0 is returned if an attempt is made to read at end-of-file.

The **read()** function tends to be very implementation dependent and may exhibit behavior slightly different from what is stated here. Check your user manual.

In some C implementations, especially those that support the proposed ANSI standard, the header information necessary to the UNIX-like file system is no longer kept in **stdio.h** but rather in its own separate file. Check your user manual.

Related functions: **open()**, **close()**, **write()**, **lseek()**

```
#include "stdio.h"
```
► **int remove(fname)**
    char *fname;

The **remove()** erases the file specified by *fname*. It returns 0 if the file was successfully deleted and a −1 if an error occurred.

Related function: **rename()**

```
#include "stdio.h"
```
► **int rename(oldfname, newfname);**
    char *oldfname, *newfname;

The **rename()** function changes the name of the file specified by *oldfname* to *newfname*. The *newfname* must not match any existing directory entry. The **rename()** function returns 0 if successful and non-zero if an error has occurred.

Related function: **remove()**

#include "stdio.h"
▶ void rewind(stream)
FILE *stream;

The **rewind()** function moves the file-position indicator to the start of the specified stream. It also clears the end-of-file and error flags associated with *stream*. It has no return value.

Related function: **fseek()**

#include "stdio.h"
▶ int scanf(format,arg-list)
char *format;

The **scanf()** is a general-purpose input routine that reads the stream **stdin**. It can read all the built-in data types and automatically convert them into the proper internal format. It is much like the reverse of **printf()**.

The control string pointed to by *format* consists of three classifications of characters:

Format specifiers
White-space characters
Non-white-space characters

The input format specifiers are preceded by a % sign and tell **scanf()** what type of data is to be read next. These codes are listed below. For example, **%s** reads a string while **%d** reads an integer. The format string is read left to right and the format codes are matched, in order, with the arguments that comprise the argument list.

A white-space character in the control string causes **scanf()** to skip over one or more white-space characters in the input stream. A white-space character is either a space, a tab, or a newline. In essence, one white-space character in the control string will cause **scanf()** to read, but not store, any number (including zero) of white-space characters up to the first non-white-space character.

A non-white-space character causes **scanf()** to read and discard a matching character. For example, **"%d,%d"** causes **scanf()** to first read an integer, then read and discard a comma, and finally read another integer. If the specified character is not found, **scanf()** will terminate.

Code	Meaning
%c	read a single character
%d	read a decimal integer
%i	read a decimal integer
%e	read a floating point number
%f	read a floating point number
%h	read a short integer
%o	read an octal number
%s	read a string
%x	read a hexadecimal number
%p	read a pointer
%n	receives an integer value equal to the number of characters read so far

All the variables used to receive values through **scanf()** must be passed by their addresses. This means that all arguments must be pointers to the variables used as arguments. This is C's way of creating a "call by reference" and it allows a function to alter the contents of an argument. For example, if you wish to read an integer into the variable **count,** you would use the following **scanf()** call.

```
scanf("%d",&count);
```

Strings will be read into character arrays, and the array name, without any index, is the address of the first element of the array. Assuming address is the name of a character array, to read a string into the character array **address,** use:

```
scanf("%s",address);
```

In this case, **address** is already a pointer and need not be preceded by the & operator.

The input data items must be separated by spaces, tabs, or newlines. Punctuation such as commas, semicolons, and the like do not count as separators. This means

```
scanf("%d%d",&r,&c);
```

will accept an input of **10 20**, but fail with **10,20**. As in **printf()**, the **scanf()** format codes are matched in order with the variables receiving the input in the argument list.

An * placed after the % and before the format code will read data of the specified type but suppress its assignment. Thus,

```
scanf("%d%*c%d",&x,&y);
```

given the input "10/20", will place the value 10 into **x**, discard the divide sign, and give **y** the value 20.

The format commands can specify a maximum field-length modifier. This is an integer number placed between the % and the format command code that limits the number of characters read for any field. For example, if you wish to read no more than 20 characters into **address,** then you would write

```
scanf("%20s",address);
```

If the input stream were greater than 20 characters, then a subsequent call to input would begin where this call left off. For example, if

1100_Parkway_Ave,_apt_2110_B

had been entered as the response to the earlier **scanf()** call, only the first 20 characters, or up to the 'p' in "apt", would have been placed into **address** because of the maximum size specifier. This means that the remaining 8 characters, "t_2110_B", have not yet been used. If another **scanf()** call is made, such as

```
scanf("%s",str);
```

then "t_2110_B" would be placed into **str**. Input for a field may terminate before the maximum field length is reached if a white space is encountered. In this case, **scanf()** moves on to the next field.

Although spaces, tabs, and newlines are used as field separators, these are read like any other character when a single character is being read. For example, with an input stream of "x y",

    scanf("%c%c%c",&a,&b,&c);
will return with the character 'x' in **a**, a space in **b**, and the character 'y' in **c**.

Be careful: any other characters in the control string—including spaces, tabs, and newlines—will be used to match and discard characters from the input stream. Any character that matches is discarded. For example, given the input stream "10t20",

    scanf("%st%s",&x,&y);
will place 10 into **x** and 20 into **y**. The 't' is discarded because of the 't' in the control string. For another example,

    scanf("%s ",name);
will *not* return until you type a character *after* you type a terminator. This is because the space after the %s has instructed **scanf()** to read and discard spaces, tabs, and newline characters.

The **scanf()** function returns a number equal to the number of fields that were successfully assigned values. This number will not include fields that were read but not assigned, using the * modifier to suppress the assignment. A return value of **EOF** is returned if an attempt is made to read at the end-of-file mark. Zero is returned if no fields were assigned.

Related functions: **printf()**, **fscanf()**

    #include "stdio.h"
▶ **void setbuf(stream, buf)**
    FILE *stream;
    char *buf;

The **setbuf()** function is used to either specify the buffer the specified stream will use, or, if called with *buf* set to null, to turn off buffering. If a programmer-defined buffer is to be specified, then it must be **BUFSIZ** characters long. **BUFSIZ** is defined in **stdio.h.** The **setbuf()** function returns no value.

Related functions: **fopen()**, **fclose()**, **setvbuf()**

```
#include "stdio.h"
```
▶ **int setvbuf(stream, buf, mode, size)**
FILE *stream;
char *buf;
int mode;
int size;

The **setvbuf()** function allows the programmer to specify the buffer, its size, and its mode for the specified stream. The character array pointed to by *buf* is used as *stream*'s buffer for I/O operations. The size of the buffer is set by *size*, and *mode* determines how buffering will be handled. If *buf* is null, no buffering will take place.

The legal values of *mode* are **_IOFBF**, **_IONBF**, and **_IOLBF**. These are defined in **stdio.h**. When the mode is set to **_IOFBF**, then full buffering will take place. This is the default setting. When set to **_IONBF**, the stream will be unbuffered regardless of the value *buf*. If mode is **_IOLBF**, then the stream will be line-buffered, which means that the buffer will be flushed each time a newline character is written for output streams; for input streams, an input request reads all characters up to a newline. In either case, the buffer is also flushed when full.

The value of *size* must be greater than 0. The **setvbuf()** function returns 0 on success, non-zero on failure.

Related function: **setbuf()**

#include "stdio.h"
▶ int sprintf(buf, format, arg-list)
char *buf, *format;

The **sprintf()** function is identical to **printf()**, except that the output generated is placed into the array pointed to by *buf*. See the **printf()** function. The return value is equal to the number of characters actually placed into the array.

Related functions: **printf()**, **fsprintf()**

#include "stdio.h"
▶ int sscanf(buf, format,arg-list)
char *buf, *format;

The **sscanf()** function is identical to **scanf()**, except that data is read from the array pointed to by *buf* rather than **stdin**. See **scanf()**.

The return value is equal to the number of fields that were actually assigned values. This number does not include fields that were skipped through the use of the * format command modifier. A value of 0 means that no fields were assigned, and **EOF** indicates that a read was attempted at the end of the string.

Related functions: **scanf()**, **fscanf()**

#include "stdio.h"
▶ long int tell(fd)
int fd;

The **tell()** function is part of the UNIX-like I/O system and is not defined by the ANSI standard. The **tell()** function returns the current value of the file position indicator associated with the file descriptor **fd**. This value will be the number of bytes the position indicator is from the start of the file. A return value of − 1L indicates an error.

In some C implementations, especially those that support the proposed ANSI standard, the header information necessary to the UNIX-like file system is no longer kept in **stdio.h** but rather in its own separate file. Check your user manual.

Related functions: **lseek()**, **open()**, **close()**, **read()**, **write()**

```
#include "stdio.h"
```
► **char *tmpnam(name)**
```
char *name;
```

The **tmpnam()** function generates a unique filename and stores it in the array pointed to by *name*. The main purpose of **tmpnam()** is to generate a temporary file name that is different from any other file in the directory.

The function may be called up to a number of times equal to **TMP_MAX**, defined in **stdio.h**. Each time it will generate a new temporary filename. A pointer to *name* is returned on success; otherwise a null pointer is returned.

Related function: **tmpfile()**

```
#include "stdio.h"
```
► **FILE *tmpfile()**

The **tmpfile()** function opens a temporary file for update and returns a pointer to the stream. The function automatically uses a unique filename to avoid conflicts with existing files. The **tmpfile()** function returns a null pointer on failure; otherwise it returns a pointer to the stream.

The temporary file created by **tmpfile()** is automatically removed when the file is closed or when the program terminates.

Related function: **tmpnam()**

```
#include "stdio.h"
```
▶ **int ungetc(ch,stream)**
   int ch;
   FILE *stream;

The **ungetc()** function returns the character specified by the low-order byte of *ch* back onto the input stream *stream*. This character will then be returned by the next read operation on *stream*. A call to **fflush()** or **fseek()** undoes an **ungetc()** operation and discards the character putback. A one-character push-back is guaranteed; however, some implementations will accept more.

You may not unget an **EOF**.

A call to **ungetc()** clears the end-of-file flag associated with the specified stream. The value of the file position indicator for a text stream is undefined until all pushed-back characters are read, in which case it will be the same as it was prior to the first **ungetc()** call. For binary streams, each **ungetc()** call decrements the file position indicator.

The return value is equal to *ch* on success and **EOF** on failure.

Related function: **getc()**

```
#include "stdio.h"
```
▶ **int unlink(fname)**
   char *fname;

The **unlink()** function is part of the UNIX-like I/O system and is not defined by the proposed ANSI standard. The **unlink()** function removes the specified file from the directory. It returns 0 on success and −1 on failure.

In some C implementations, especially those that support the proposed ANSI standard, the header information necessary to the UNIX-like file system is no longer kept in **stdio.h** but rather in its own separate file. Check your user manual.

Related functions: **open()**, **close()**

```
#include "stdarg.h"
#include "stdio.h"
```
▶ **int vprintf(format, arg_ptr)**
```
char *format;
va_list arg_ptr;
```
▶ **int vfprintf(stream, format, arg_ptr)**
```
FILE *stream;
char *format;
va_list arg_ptr;
```
▶ **int vsprintf(buf, format, arg_ptr)**
```
char *buf;
char *format;
va_list arg_ptr;
```

The functions **vprintf()**, **vfprintf()**, and **vsprintf()** are functionally equivalent to **printf()**, **fprintf()**, and **sprintf()**, respectively, except that the argument list has been replaced by a pointer to a list of arguments. This pointer must be of type **va_list** and is defined in **stdarg.h.**

Related functions: **va_list()**, **va_start()**, **va_end()**

```
#include "stdio.h"
```
▶ **int write(fd,buf,count)**
```
int fd;
char *buf;
unsigned int count;
```

The **write()** function is part of the UNIX-like I/O system and is not defined by the proposed ANSI standard. The **write()** function writes *count* number of bytes to the file described by *fd* from the buffer pointed to by *buf*. The file-position indicator is adjusted forward by the number of bytes written. If the file is opened in text mode, then character translations may take place.

The return value will be equal to the number of bytes actually written. This number may be smaller than *count* if an error is encountered. A value of -1 means an error has occurred.

The **write()** function tends to be very implementation dependent and may exhibit behavior slightly different than stated here. Check your user manual.

In some C implementations, especially those that support the proposed ANSI standard, the header information necessary to the UNIX-like file system is no longer kept in **stdio.h** but rather in its own separate file. Check your user manual.

Related functions: **read()**, **close()**, **write()**, **lseek()**

STRING AND CHARACTER FUNCTIONS

The C standard library has a rich and varied set of string- and character-handling functions. In C, a string is a null terminated array of characters. In an ANSI standard implementation, the string functions require the header file **strings.h** to provide their declarations. The character functions use **ctype.h** as their header file. These files may have different names if the compiler does not follow the proposed ANSI standard.

Because C has no bounds checking on array operations, it is the programmer's responsibility to prevent an array overflow. As the proposed ANSI standard puts it, if an array has overflowed, "the behavior is undefined"—which is a nice way of saying that your program is about to crash!

In C, a *printable character* is one that can be displayed on a termimal. These are usually the characters between a space (0x20) and tilde (0xfE). *Control characters* have values between (0) and (0x1F) as well as DEL (0x7F).

The character functions are declared to take an integer argument. While this is true, only the low-order byte is used by the function. Generally, you are free to use a character argument because it will automatically be elevated to **int** at the time of the call.

The functions are described as defined by the proposed ANSI standard and are compatible with those provided with virtually all existing C compilers. However, if your compiler does not support **void** pointers, you will have to substitute **char** pointers for the memory-related functions such as **memmove**() and the like. As with many functions in the standard library, the header files **string.h** and **ctype.h** may be optional if strong type checking is not desired.

```
#include "ctype.h"
```
▶ **int isalnum(ch);**
```
int ch;
```

The **isalnum()** function returns non-zero if its argument is either a letter of the alphabet or a digit. If the character is not an alphanumeric, then 0 is returned.

Related functions: **isalpha()**, **isdigit()**, **iscntrl()**, **isgraph()**, **isprint()**, **ispunct()**, **isspace()**

```
#include "ctype.h"
```
▶ **int isalpha(ch)**
```
int ch;
```

The **isalpha()** function returns non-zero if *ch* is a letter of the alphabet; otherwise 0 is returned.

Related functions: **isalnum()**, **isdigit()**, **iscntrl()**, **isgraph()**, **isprint()**, **ispunct()**, **isspace()**

```
#include "ctype.h"
```
▶ **int iscntrl(ch)**
```
int ch;
```

The **iscntrl()** function returns non-zero if *ch* is between 0 and 0x1F or is equal to 0x7F (DEL); otherwise 0 is returned.

Related functions: **isalnum()**, **isdigit()**, **isalpha()**, **isgraph()**, **isprint()**, **ispunct()**, **isspace()**

```
#include "ctype.h"
```
▶ **int isdigit(ch)**
```
int ch;
```

The **isdigit()** function returns non-zero if *ch* is a digit, that is, '0' through '9'. Otherwise 0 is returned.

Related functions: **isalnum()**, **iscntrl()**, **isalpha()**, **isgraph()**, **isprint()**, **ispunct()**, **isspace()**

#include "ctype.h"
▶ **int isgraph(ch)**
int ch;

The **isgraph()** function returns non-zero if *ch* is any printable character other than a space; otherwise 0 is returned. Although printable characters are implementation dependent, they are generally in the range 0x21 through 0x7E.

Related functions: **isalnum()**, **iscntrl()**, **isalpha()**, **isdigit()**, **isprint()**, **ispunct()**, **isspace()**

#include "ctype.h"
▶ **int islower(ch)**
int ch;

The **islower()** function returns non-zero if *ch* is a lowercase letter ('a'-'z'); otherwise 0 is returned.

Related functions: **isupper()**

#include "ctype.h"
▶ **int isprint(ch)**
int ch;

The **isprint()** function returns non-zero if *ch* is a printable character, including a space; otherwise 0 is returned. Although printable characters are implementation dependent, they are often in the range 0x20 through 0x7E.

Related functions: **isalnum()**, **iscntrl()**, **isalpha()**, **isdigit()**, **isgraph()**, **ispunct()**, **isspace()**

#include "ctype.h"
▶ int ispunct(ch)
int ch;

The **ispunct()** function returns non-zero if *ch* is a punctuation character, excluding the space; otherwise 0 is returned. The term "punctuation," as defined by this function, includes all printing characters that are neither alphanumeric nor a space.

Related functions: **isalnum()**, **iscntrl()**, **isalpha()**, **isdigit()**, **isgraph()**, **ispunct()**, **isspace()**

#include "ctype.h"
▶ int isspace(ch)
int ch;

The **isspace()** function returns non-zero if *ch* is either a space, tab, or newline charcter; otherwise 0 is returned.

Related functions: **isalnum()**, **iscntrl()**, **isalpha()**, **isdigit()**, **isgraph()**, **isspace()**, **ispunct()**

#include "ctype.h"
▶ int isupper(ch)
int ch;

The **isupper()** function returns non-zero if *ch* is an uppercase letter ('A'-'Z'); otherwise 0 is returned.

Related function: **islower()**

#include "ctype.h"
▶ int isxdigit(ch)
int ch;

The **isxdigit()** function returns non-zero if *ch* is a hexadecimal digit; otherwise 0 is returned. A hexadecimal digit will be in one of these ranges: 'A'-'F', 'a'-'f', or '0'-'9'.

Related functions: **isalnum()**, **iscntrl()**, **isalpha()**, **is-digit()**, **isgraph()**, **isspace()**, **ispunct()**

```
#include "string.h"
```
 void *memchr(buffer, ch, count)
```
void *buffer;
int ch;
unsigned int count;
```

The **memchr()** function searches *buffer* for the first occurrence of *ch* in the first *count* characters. The **memchr()** function returns a pointer to the first occurrence of *ch* in *buffer*, or a null pointer if *ch* is not found. For compilers that do not support **void**, **char** pointers are substituted.

Related functions: **memmove()**, **memcpy()**

```
#include "string.h"
```
 int memcmp(buf1, buf2, count)
```
void *buf1;
void *buf2;
unsigned int count;
```

The **memcmp()** functions compares the first *count* characters of the arrays pointed to by *buf1* and *buf2*. The comparison is done lexicographically. The **memcmp()** function returns an integer that is interpreted as follows:

Value	Meaning
less than 0	buf1 is less than buf2
0	buf1 is equal to buf2
greater than 0	buf1 is greater than buf2

For compilers that do not support **void**, **char** pointers are substituted.

Related functions: **memcpy()**, **memchr()**, **strcmp()**

77

```
#include "string.h"
```
► **void *memcpy(to, from, count)**
```
void *to;
void *from;
unsigned int count;
```

The **memcpy()** function copies *count* characters from the array pointed to by *from* into the array pointed to by *to*. If the arrays overlap, the behavior of **memcopy()** is undefined. The **memcpy()** function returns a pointer to *to*. For compilers that do not support **void, char** pointers are substituted.

Related function: **memmove()**

```
#include "string.h"
```
► **void *memmove(to, from, count)**
```
void *to;
void *from;
unsigned int count;
```

The **memmove()** function copies *count* characters from the array pointed to by *from* into the array pointed to by *to*. If the arrays overlap, the copy will take place correctly, placing the correct contents into *to* but leaving *from* modified. The **memmove()** function returns a pointer to *to*. For compilers that do not support **void, char** pointers are substituted.

Related function: **memcpy()**

```
#include "string.h"
```
► **void *memset(buf, ch, count)**
```
void *buf;
int ch;
unsigned int count;
```

The **memset()** function copies the low-order byte of *ch* into the first *count* characters of the array pointed to by *buf*. It returns *buf*. The most common use of **memset()** is to initialize a region of memory to some known value. For compilers that do not support **void**, **char** pointers are substituted.

Related functions: **memcpy()**, **memcmp()**, **mem-move()**

```
#include "string.h"
char *strcat(str1, str2)
char *str1, *str2;
```

The **strcat()** function concatenates a copy of *str2* to *str1* and terminates *str1* with a null. The null terminator originally ending *str1* is overwritten by the first character of *str2*. The string *str2* is untouched by the operation. The **strcat()** function returns *str1*.

Remember, no bounds checking takes place, so the programmer must ensure that *str1* is large enough to hold both its original contents as well as those of *str2*.

Related functions: **strchr()**, **strcmp()**, **strcpy()**

```
#include "string.h"
char *strchr(str, ch)
char *str;
int ch;
```

The **strchr()** function returns a pointer to the first occurrence of the low-order byte of *ch* in the string pointed to by *str*. If no match is found, a null pointer is returned.

Related functions: **strpbrk()**, **strstr()**, **strtok()**, **strspn()**

```
#include "string.h"
```
▶ **unsigned int strcoll(to, count, from)**
```
char *to;
unsigned int count;
char *from;
```

The *strcoll* function is used to adjust the string pointed to by *from* so that it can be ordered by **memcmp()** or **strcmp()** as is required by the specific situation. The outcome of such adjustment is placed into the string pointed to by *to*, up to the length specified by *count*. At no time, however, will the length of the string pointed to by *to* ever exceed twice that of the length of the string pointed to by *from*. The **strcoll()** function returns the length of *to* if successful, and 0 if not. For most applications, **strcoll()** will never be used.

Related functions: **memcmp()**, **strcmp()**

```
#include "string.h"
```
▶ **int strcmp(str1,str2)**
```
char *str1,*str2;
```

The **strcmp()** function lexicographically compares two null terminated strings and returns an integer based on the outcome, as shown here.

Value	Meaning
less than 0	str1 is less than str2
0	str1 is equal to str2
greater than 0	str1 is greater than str2

Related functions: **strchr()**, **strcmp()**, **strcpy()**, **strncmp()**

```
#include "string.h"
```
▶ **char *strcpy(str1,str2)**
```
char *str1,*str2;
```

The **strcpy()** function is used to copy the contents of *str2* into *str1*. *Str2* must be a pointer to a null terminated string. The **strcpy()** function returns a pointer to *str1*. If *str1* and *str2* overlap, the behavior of **strcpy()** is undefined.

Related functions: **strchr()**, **strcmp()**, **memcpy()**, **strncmp()**

#include "stdio.h"
▶ **int strcspn(str1, str2)**
char *str1, *str2;

The **strcspn()** function returns the length of the initial substring of the string pointed to by *str1* that is made up of only those characters not contained in the string pointed to by *str2*. In other words, **strcspn()** returns the index of the first character in the string pointed to by *str1* that matches any of the characters in the string pointed to by *str2*. Related functions: **strpbrk()**, **strstr()**, **strtok()**, **strrchr()**

#include "string.h"
▶ **char *strerror(errnum)**
int errnum;

The **strerror()** function maps the specified error number onto an error-message string. It returns a pointer to the string. The actual message associated with each *errnum* is implementation defined. However, under no circumstances should you modify the string.

#include "string.h"
▶ **unsigned int strlen(str)**
char *str;

The **strlen()** function returns the length of the null terminated string pointed to by *str*. The null is not counted.

Related functions: **strchr()**, **strcmp()**, **memcpy()**, **strncmp()**

#include "string.h"

▶ **char *strncat(str1, str2, count)**
char *str1, *str2;
unsigned int count;

The **strncat** function concatenates not more than *count* characters of the string pointed to by *str2* to the string pointed to by *str1* and terminates *str1* with a null. The null terminator originally ending *str1* is overwritten by the first character of *str2*. The string *str2* is untouched by the operation. The **strncat()** function returns *str1*.

Remember, no bounds checking takes place, so the programmer must ensure that *str1* is large enough to hold both its original contents as well as those of *str2*.

Related functions: **strnchr()**, **strncmp()**, **strncpy()**, **strcat()**

#include "string.h"

▶ **int strncmp(str1,str2,count)**
char *str1,*str2;
unsigned int count;

The **strncmp()** function lexicographically compares not more than *count* characters from the two null terminated strings and returns an integer based on the outcome, as shown here.

Value	Meaning
less than 0	str1 is less than str2
0	str1 is equal to str2
greater than 0	str1 is greater than str2

If there are fewer than *count* characters in either string, then the comparison ends when the first null is encountered.

Related functions: **strnchr()**, **strcmp()**, **strncpy()**

#include "string.h"
► char *strncpy(str1,str2, count)
char *str1,*str2;

The **strncpy()** function is used to copy up to *count* characters from the string pointed to by *str2* into the string pointed to by *str1*. *Str2* must be a pointer to a null terminated string. The **strncpy()** function returns a pointer to *str1*. If *str1* and *str2* overlap, the behavior of **strncpy()** is undefined.

If the string pointed to by *str2* has less than *count* characters, then nulls will be appended to the end of *str1* until *count* characters have been copied. Alternately, if the string pointed to by *str2* is longer than count characters, then the resultant string pointed to by *str1* will not be null terminated.

Related functions: **strchr()**, **strncmp()**, **memcpy()**, **strncat()**

#include "string.h"
► char *strpbrk(str1,str2)
char *str1, *str2;

The **strpbrk()** function returns a pointer to the first character in the string pointed to by *str1* that matches any character in the string pointed to by *str2*. The null terminators are not included. If there are no matches, a null pointer is returned.

Related functions: **strrchr()**, **strstr()**, **strtok()**, **strspn()**

#include "string.h"
► char *strrchr(str, ch)
char *str;
int ch;

The **strrchr()** function returns a pointer to the last occurrence of the low-order byte of *ch* in the string pointed to by *str*. If no match is found, a null pointer is returned.

Related functions: **strpbrk()**, **strstr()**, **strtok()**, **strspn()**

#include "stdio.h"
▶ int strspn(str1, str2)
char *str1, *str2;

The **strspn()** function returns the length of the initial substring of the string pointed to by *str1* that is made up of only those characters contained in the string pointed to by *str2*. In other words, **strspn()** returns the index of the first character in the string pointed to by *str1* that does not match any of the characters in the string pointed to by *str2*.

Related functions: **strpbrk()**, **strstr()**, **strtok()**, **strrchr()**

#include "stdio.h"
▶ char *strstr(str1, str2)
char *str1, *str2;

The **strstr()** function returns a pointer to the first occurrence in the string pointed to by *str1* of the string pointed to by *str2* (except *str2*'s null terminator). It returns a null pointer if no match is found.

Related functions: **strpbrk()**, **strspn()**, **strtok()**, **strrchr()**, **strchr()**, **strcspn()**

#include "string.h"
▶ char *strtok(str1, str2)
char *str1, *str2;

The **strtok()** function returns a pointer to the next token in the string pointed to by *str1*. The characters making up the string pointed to by *str2* are the delimiters that determine the token. A null pointer is returned when there is no token to return. The first time **strtok()** is called, *str1* is actually used in the call. Subsequent calls use a null pointer for the first argument. In this way the entire string can be reduced to its tokens.

It is important to understand that the **strtok()** function modifies the string pointed to by *str1*. Each time a token is found, a null is placed where the delimiter was found. In this way, **strtok()** can continue to advance through the string. It is possible to use a different set of delimiters for each call to **strtok()**.

Related functions: **strpbrk()**, **strspn()**, **strtok()**, **strrchr()**, **strchr()**, **strcspn()**

#include "ctype.h"
► **int tolower(ch)**
int ch;

The **tolower** function returns the lowercase equivalent of *ch* if *ch* is a letter; otherwise *ch* is returned unchanged.

Related functions: **toupper()**

#include "ctype.h"
► **int toupper(ch)**
int ch;

The **toupper** function returns the uppercase equivalent of *ch* if *ch* is a letter; otherwise *ch* is returned unchanged.

MATHEMATICAL FUNCTIONS

The proposed ANSI standard defines 22 functions that take **double** arguments and return **double** values. These functions fall into the following categories:

Trigonometric functions
Hyperbolic functions
Exponential and logarithmic functions
Miscellaneous

Even if your compiler is not completely standard, the math functions described here will most likely be applicable.

All the math functions require the header **math.h** to be included in any program using them. In addition to declaring the math functions, this header defines three macros called **EDOM**, **ERANGE**, and **HUGE_VAL**. If an argument to a math function is not in the domain for which it is defined, then an implementation-defined value is returned and the global **errno** is set equal to **EDOM**. If a routine produces a result that is too large to be represented by a **double**, then an overflow occurs. This causes the routine to return **HUGE_VAL** and **errno** is set to **ERANGE**, indicating a range error. If an underflow happens, the routine returns 0 and sets **errno** to **ERANGE**. If your compiler does not agree with the proposed ANSI standard, the exact operation of the routines in error situations may be different.

#include "math.h"

► **double acos(arg)**
 double arg;

The **acos()** function returns the arc cosine of *arg*. The argument to **acos()** must be in the range −1 to 1; otherwise a domain error will occur.

Related functions: **asin()**, **atan()**, **atan2()**, **sin()**, **cos()**, **tan()**, **sinh()**, **cosh()**, **tanh()**

```
#include "math.h"
```
▶ **double asin(arg)**
   double arg;

The **asin()** function returns the arc sine of *arg*. The argument to **asin()** must be in the range -1 to 1; otherwise a domain error will occur.

Related functions: **asin()**, **atan()**, **atan2()**, **sin()**, **cos()**, **tan()**, **sinh()**, **cosh()**, **tanh()**

```
#include "math.h"
```
▶ **double atan(arg)**
   double arg;

The **atan()** function returns the arc tangent of *arg*.

Related functions: **asin()**, **acos()**, **atan2()**, **tan()**, **cos()**, **sin()**, **sinh()**, **cosh()**, **tanh()**

```
#include "math.h"
```
▶ **double atan2(y,x)**
   double y,x;

The **atan2()** function returns the arc tangent of y/x. It uses the signs of its arguments to compute the quadrand of the return value.

Related functions: **asin()**, **acos()**, **atan()**, **tan()**, **cos()**, **sin()**, **sinh()**, **cosh()**, **tanh()**

```
#include "math.h"
```
▶ **double ceil(num)**
   double num;

The **ceil()** function returns the smallest integer (represented as a **double**) not less than *num*. For example, given 1.02, **ceil()** would return 2.0. Given -1.02, **ceil()** would return -1.

Related functions: **floor()**, **fmod()**

#include "math.h"
▶ **double cos(arg)**
double arg;

The **cos()** function returns the cosine of *arg*. The value of *arg* must be in radians.

Related functions: **asin()**, **acos()**, **atan2()**, **atan()**, **tan()**, **sin()**, **sinh()**, **cosh()**, **tanh()**

#include "math.h"
▶ **double cosh(arg)**
double arg;

The **cosh()** function returns the hyperbolic cosine of *arg*. The value of *arg* must be in radians.

Related functions: **asin()**, **acos()**, **atan2()**, **atan()**, **tan()**, **sin()**, **cosh()**, **tanh()**

#include "math.h"
▶ **double exp(arg)**
double arg;

The **exp()** function returns the natural logarithm *e* raised to the *arg* power.

Related function: **log()**

#include "math.h"
▶ **double fabs(num)**
double num;

The **fabs()** function returns the absolute value of *num*.

Related function: **abs()**

#include "math.h"
▶ double floor(num)
double num;

The **floor()** function returns the largest integer (represented as a **double**) not greater than *num*. For example, given 1.02, **floor()** would return 1.0. Given -1.02, **floor()** would return -2.0.

Related functions: **fceil()**, **fmod()**

#include "math.h"
▶ double fmod(x,y)
double x,y;

The **fmod()** function returns the remainder of x/y.

Related functions: (**ceil()**, **floor()**, **fabs()**)

#include "math.h"
▶ double frexp(num, exp)
double num;
int *exp;

The **frexp()** function decomposes the number *num* into a mantissa in the range 0.5 to less than 1, and an integer exponent such that $num = mantissa * 2^{exp}$. The mantissa is returned by the function and the exponent is stored at the variable pointed to by *exp*.

Related functions: **ldexp()**

#include "math.h"
▶ double ldexp(num, exp)
double num;
int exp;

The **ldexp()** returns the value of $num * 2^{exp}$. If overflow occurs, **HUGE_VAL** is returned.

Related functions: **frexp()**, **modf()**

#include "math.h"
▶ double log(num)
double num;

The **log()** function returns the natural logarithm for *num*. A domain error occurs if *num* is negative, and a range error occurs if the argument is 0.

Related function: **log10()**

#include "math.h"
▶ double log10(num)
double num;

The **log10()** function returns the base 10 logarithm for *num*. A domain error occurs if *num* is negative, and a range error occurs if the argument is 0.

Related function: **log()**

#include "math.h"
▶ double modf(num, i)
double num;
int *i;

The **modf()** function decomposes *num* into its integer and fractional parts. It returns the fractional portion and places the integer part in the variable pointed to by *i*.

Related functions: **frexp()**, **ldexp()**

#include "math.h"
▶ double pow(base, exp)
double base, exp;

The **pow()** function returns *base* raised to the *exp* power *(base^{exp})*. A domain error occurs if *base* is 0 and *exp* is less than or equal to 0. It may also happen if *base* is negative and *exp* is not an integer. An overflow produces a range error.

Related functions: **exp()**, **log()**, **sqrt()**

#include "math.h"
▶ **double sin(arg)**
  double arg;

The **sin()** function returns the sine of *arg*. The value of *arg* must be in radians.

Related functions: **asin()**, **acos()**, **atan2()**, **atan()**, **tan()**, **cos()**, **sinh()**, **cosh()**, **tanh()**

#include "math.h"
▶ **double sinh(arg)**
  double arg;

The **sinh()** function returns the hyperbolic sine of *arg*. The value of *arg* must be in radians.

Related functions: **asin()**, **acos()**, **atan2()**, **atan()**, **tan()**, **cos()**, **tanh()**, **cosh()**

#include "math.h"
▶ **double sqrt(num)**
  double num;

The **sqrt()** function returns the square root of *num*. If called with a negative argument, a domain error will occur.

Related functions: **exp()**, **log()**, **pow()**

#include "math.h"
▶ **double tan(arg)**
  double arg;

The **tan()** function returns the tangent of *arg*. The value of *arg* must be in radians.

Related functions: **asin()**, **atan()**, **atan2()**, **atan()**, **cos()**, **sin()**, **sinh()**, **cosh()**, **tanh()**

#include "math.h"
▶ **double tanh(arg)**
double arg;

The **tanh()** function returns the hyperbolic tangent of arg. The value of arg must be in radians.

Related functions: **asin()**, **atan()**, **atan2()**, **atan()**, **cos()**, **sin()**, **cosh()**, **sin()**

TIME, DATE, AND OTHER SYSTEM RELATED FUNCTIONS

This section covers those functions that in one way or another are more operating-system sensitive than others. Of the functions defined by the proposed ANSI standard, these include the time and date functions as well as **setlocale()**. These functions relate to the operating system by using its time and date information or, as with **setlocale()**, its geographic information.

This section also discusses a category of functions that allow direct operating-system interfacing. None of these functions is defined by the proposed ANSI standard because each operating environment is different. Therefore, it is only possible to discuss representative functions for one specific operating system: PC-DOS. PC-DOS is choosen because it is one of the most widely used operating systems.

The proposed ANSI standard defines several functions that deal with the date and time of the system as well as elapsed time. These functions require the header **time.h** for the declarations and also define three types. The types **clock_t** and **time_t** are capable of representing the system time and date as a long integer. The proposed ANSI standard refers to this as calendar *time*. The structure type **tm** holds the date and time broken down into its elements. The **tm** structure is defined as follows.

```
struct tm {
    int tm_sec;      seconds, 0-59
    int tm_min;      minutes, 0-59
    int tm_hour;     hours, 0-23
    int tm_mday;     day of the month, 1-31
    int tm_mon;      months since Jan, 0-11
    int tm_year;     years from 1900
    int tm_wday;     days since Sunday, 0-6
    int tm_yday;     days since Jan 1, 0-365
    int tm_isdst     Daylight Savings Time indicator
}
```

The value of **tm_isdst** will be positive if Daylight Savings
Time is in effect, 0 if it is not in effect, and negative if
no information is available. The proposed ANSI standard
refers to this form of the time and date as *broken-down
time*.

In addition, **time.h** defines the macro **CLK_TCK**,
which is the number of system clock ticks per second.
The **setlocale**() function requires the header **locale.h**.

The PCDOS interfacing functions require the header
dos.h. The file **dos.h** defines a union that corresponds
to the registers of the 8088/86 CPU and is used by some
of the system-interfacing functions. It is defined as the
union of two structures in order to allow each register to
be accessed either by word or byte. The Turbo C version
of this union is shown here, but most compilers use the
same format.

```
struct WORDREGS
    {
    unsigned int ax, bx, cx, dx, si, di, cflag;
    };

struct BYTEREGS
    {
    unsigned char al, ah, bl, bh, cl, ch, dl, dh;
    };

union REGS {
    struct WORDREGS x;
    struct BYTEREGS h;
    };
```

```
#include "time.h"
```
▶ **char *asctime(ptr);**
  strcut tm *ptr;

The **asctime()** function returns a pointer to a string that
converts the information stored in the structure pointed
to by *ptr* into the following form:

  day month date hours:minutes:seconds year/n/0

For example:

  Wed Jun 19 12:05:34 1999

The structure pointer passed to **asctime()** is generally
obtained from either **localtime()** or **gmtime()**.

The buffer used by **asctime()** to hold the formatted
output string is a statically allocated character array and
is overwritten each time the function is called. If you
wish to save the contents of the string, you must copy
it elsewhere.

Related functions: **localtime()**, **gmtime()**, **time()**,
ctime()

```
#include "dos.h"
```
▶ **int bdos(fnum, dx, al)**
  int fnum;
  unsigned dx, al;

This function is not part of the proposed ANSI standard.
The **bdos()** function is used to access the PC-DOS system
call specified by *fnum*. It first places the values *dx* into
the *DX* register and *al* into the *AL* register and then
executes an INT 21H instruction.

The **bdos()** function returns the value of the *AX* register, which is used by PC-DOS to return information.
The **bdos()** function can only be used to access those

system calls that either take no arguments or require only
DX and/or *AL* for their arguments.

Related functions: **intdos()**, **intdosx()**

   #include "time.h"
▶ **clock_t clock();**

The **clock()** function returns a value that approximates
the amount of time the calling program has been running.
To transform this value into seconds, divide it by
CLK_TCK. A value of -1 is returned if the time is
not available.

Related functions: **time()**, **asctime()**, **ctime()**

   #include "time.h"
▶ **char *ctime(time)**
   long *time;

The **ctime()** function returns a pointer to a string of the
form

   day month date hours:minutes:seconds year/n/0

given a pointer to the calendar time. The calendar time
is generally obtained through a call to **time()**.

The buffer used by **ctime()** to hold the formatted output string is a statically allocated character array and is
overwritten each time the function is called. If you wish
to save the contents of the string, you must copy it elsewhere.

Related functions: **localtime()**, **gmtime()**, **time()**,
asctime()

   #include "time.h"
▶ **double difftime(time2, time1)**
   time_t time2, time1;

The **difftime()** function returns the difference, in seconds, between *time1* and *time2*. That is, *time2 − time1*.

Related functions: **localtime()**, **gmtime()**, **time()**, **asctime()**

#include "time.h"
▶ **struct tm *gmtime(time)**
time_t *time;

The **gmtime()** returns a pointer to the broken-down form of *time* in the form of a **tm** structure. The time is represented in Greenwich mean time. The *time* value is generally obtained through a call to **time()**.

The structure used by **gmtime()** to hold the broken-down time is statically allocated and is overwritten each time the function is called. If you wish to save the contents of the structure, it is necessary to copy it elsewhere.

Related functions: **localtime()**, **time()**, **asctime()**

#include "dos.h"
▶ **int int86(int_num, in_regs,
out_regs);**
int int_num;
union REGS *in_regs, *out_regs;

The **int86()** function is not part of the proposed ANSI standard. The **int86()** function is used to execute a software interrupt specified by *int_num*. The contents of the union *in_regs* are first copied into the register of the processor and then the proper interrupt is executed.

Upon return, the union *out_regs* will contain the values of the registers that the CPU has upon return from the interrupt. The union **REGS** is defined in the header **dos.h**.

Related functions: **intdos()**, **bdos()**

#include "dos.h"

▶ int intdos(in_regs, out_regs)
union REGS *in_regs, *out_regs;

The **intdos()** function is not part of the proposed ANSI standard. The **intdos()** function is used to access the DOS system call specified by the contents of the union pointed to by *in_regs*. It executes an INT 21H instruction and the outcome of the operation is placed in the union pointed to by *out_regs*. The **intdos()** function returns the value of the *AX* register, which is used by PC-DOS to return information.

The **intdos()** function is used to access those system calls that either require arguments in registers other than only *DX* and/or *AL* or that return information in a register other than *AX*.

The union **REGS** defines the registers of the 8088/86 family of processors and is found in the **dos.h** header file.

Related functions: **bdos()**, **int86()**

#include "time.h"

▶ struct tm *localtime(time)
time_t *time;

The **localtime()** function returns a pointer to the broken-down form of *time* in the form of a **tm** structure. The time is represented in local time. The *time* value is generally obtained through a call to **time()**. The structure used by **localtime()** to hold the broken-down time is statically allocated and is overwritten each time the function is called. If you wish to save the contents of the structure, you must copy it elsewhere.

Related functions: **gmtime()**, **time()**, **asctime()**

```
#include "time.h"
```
▶ **time_t mktime(time)**
   struct tm *time;

The **mktime()** function returns the calendar time equivalent of the broken-down time found in the structure pointed to by *time*. This function is primarily used to initialize the system time. The elements **tm_wday** and **tm_yday** are set by the function, so they need not be defined at the time of the call.

If **mktime()** cannot represent the information as a valid calendar time, a − 1 is returned.

Related functions: **time()**, **gmtime()**, **asctime()**, **ctime()**

```
#include "locale.h"
```
▶ **char *setlocale(category, locale)**
   int category;
   char *locale;

The **setlocale()** function allows certain parameters that are sensitive to the geo-political location of a program's execution to be queried or set. For example, in Europe, the comma is used in place of the decimal point.

If *locale* is null, then **setlocale()** returns a pointer to the current localization string. Otherwise, **setlocale()** attempts to use the specified localization string to set the locale parameters as specified by the *category*.

At the time of the call, *category* must be one of the following macros:

LC_ALL
LC_COLLATE
LC_CTYPE
LC_NUMERIC
LC_TIME

LC_ALL refers to all localization categories. **LC_COL-**

LATE affects the operation of the **strcoll()** function.
LC_CTYPE alters the way the character functions work.
LC_NUMERIC changes the decimal-point character for
formatted input/output functions. Finally, **LC_TIME** determines the behavior of the **strftime()** funtion.

The standard defines two possible strings for *locale*.
The first is **"C"**, which specifies a minimal environment
for C compilation. The second is **" "**, the null string,
which specifies the implementation-defined default environment. All other values for **locale()** are implementation
defined and will affect portability.

Related functions: **time()**, **strcoll()**, **strftime()**

#include "time.h"
► **size_t strftime(str, maxsize, fmt, time)**
char *str;
size_t maxsize;
char *fmt;
struct tm *time;

The **strftime()** function places time and date information,
along with other information, into the string pointed to
by *str* according to the format commands found in the
string pointed to by *fmt* and using the broken-down time
time. A maximum of *maxsize* characters will be placed
into *str*.

The **strftime()** function works a little like **sprintf()**
in that it (1) recognizes a set of format commands that
begin with the percent sign (%), and (2) places its formatted output into a string. The format commands are
used to specify the exact way various time and date
information is represented in *str*. Any other characters
found in the format string are placed into *str* unchanged.
The time and date displayed are in local time. The format

commands are shown below. Notice that many of the commands are case sensitive.

The **strftime()** function returns the number of characters placed in the string pointed to by *str*, or 0 if an error occurs.

Command	Replaced by
%a	abbreviated weekday name
%A	full weekday name
%b	abbreviated month name
%B	full month name
%c	standard date and time string
%d	day-of-month as a decimal (1-31)
%H	hour, range (0-23)
%I	hour, range (1-12)
%j	day-of-year as a decimal (1-366)
%m	month as decimal (1-12)
%M	minute as decimal (0-59)
%p	locale's equivalent of AM or PM
%S	second as decimal (0-59)
%U	week-of-year, Sunday being first day (0-52)
%w	weekday as a decimal (0-6, Sunday being 0)
%W	week-of-year, Monday being first day (0-52)
%x	standard date string
%X	standard time string
%y	year in decimal without century (00-99)
%Y	year including century as decimal
%Z	time zone name
%%	the percent sign

Related functions: **time()**, **localtime()**, **gmtime()**

#include "time.h"
► **time_t time(time)**
time_t time;

The **time()** function returns the current calendar time of
the system. If the system has no time then −1 is returned.
The **time()** function can be called either with a null pointer
or with a pointer to a variable of type **time_t**. If the
latter is used, then the argument will also beassigned the
calendar time.

Related functions: **localtime()**, **gmtime()**, **strftime()**,
ctime()

DYNAMIC ALLOCATION

There are two primary ways in which a C program can store information in the main memory of the computer. The first uses *global* and *local* variables, including arrays and structures. In the case of **global** and **static** local variables, the storage is fixed throughout the runtime of your program. For **dynamic** local variables, storage is allocated from the stack space of the computer. Although these variables are efficiently implemented in C, they require the programmer to know in advance the amount of storage needed for every situation. The second way that information can be stored is through the use of C's dynamic allocation system. In this method, storage for information is allocated from the free-memory area as it is needed. The free-memory region lies between your program and its permanent storage area, and the stack. (For the 8086 family of processors, the heap is thought of as being in the default data segment.) The stack grows downward as it is used, so the amount of memory it needs is determined by how your program is designed. For example, a program with many recursive functions will make much greater demands on stack memory than one that does not have recursive functions because local variables are stored on the stack. The memory required for the program and global data is fixed during the execution of the program. Memory to satisfy an allocation request is taken from the free–memory area, starting just above the global variables and growing towards the stack. As you might guess, it is possible, under fairly extreme cases, for the stack to run into the heap.

At the core of C's dynamic allocation system are the functions **malloc()** and **free()**, which are part of the standard C library. Each time a **malloc()** memory request is made, a portion of the remaining free memory is allocated. Each time a **free()** memory release call is made, memory is returned to the system. The most common way to implement **malloc()** and **free()** is to organize the free memory into a linked list. However, the proposed ANSI standard explicitly states that the memory-management method is implementation dependent.

The proposed ANSI standard specifies that the header information necessary to the dynamic allocation system will be in **stdlib.h**. However, at the time of this writing, a great many C compilers require you to include the header **malloc.h** instead. This guide will use the proposed standard's approach, but you may need to do otherwise, based upon the compiler you are using.

The proposed ANSI standard specifies that the dynamic allocation system returns **void** pointers, which are considered *generic* (they may point to any object). However, many compilers return a **char** pointer. In either case, you should use an explicit type cast when assigning them to pointers of other types.

The proposed ANSI standard defines only four functions for the dynamic allocation system: **calloc()**, **malloc()**, **free()**, and **realloc()**. However, this reference covers several others that are in wide use. Some of these additional functions are necessary to efficiently support the segmented architecture of the 8088 family of processors and will not relate to compilers designed for other processors, such as the 68000. Because of the segmented memory of the 8088 family of processors, two new, nonstandard-type modifiers are generally supported by compilers built for these processors. These modifiers are **near** and **far**, which are used to create pointers of a type other than that normally used by the memory model of the compiler.

> #include "malloc.h"
> ▶ **char *alloca(size)**
> unsigned int size;

The **alloca()** function is not defined by the proposed ANSI standard. The **alloca()** function allocates *size* bytes of memory from the system stack (not the heap) and returns a character pointer to it. A null pointer is returned if the allocation request cannot be honored.

Memory allocated using **alloca()** is automatically released when the function that called **alloca()** returns. This means that you should never use a pointer generated by **alloca()** as an argument to **free()**.

Related functions: **malloc()**, **stackavail()**

▶ #include "stdlib.h"
void *calloc(num, size);
unsigned int num;
unsigned int size;

The **calloc()** function returns a pointer to the allocated memory. The amount of memory allocated is equal to *num*size*. That is, **calloc()** allocates sufficient memory for an array of *num* objects of size *size*.

The **calloc()** function returns a pointer to the first byte of the allocated region. If there is not enough memory to satisfy the request, a null pointer is returned. It is always important to verify that the return value is not a null pointer before attempting to use it.

Related functions: **malloc()**, **realloc()**, **free()**

▶ #include "malloc.h"
_ffree(ptr);
char far *ptr;

The **_ffree()** function is not defined by the proposed ANSI standard. The **_ffree()** function returns the memory pointed to by the **far** pointer *ptr* back to the system. This makes the memory available for future allocation. The pointer must have previously been allocated using **_fmalloc()**.

It is imperative that **_ffree()** only be called with a pointer that was previously allocated using **_fmalloc()**— it cannot free pointers allocated using other allocation functions. Using an invalid pointer in the call will probably destroy the memory-management mechanism and cause a system crash.

Related functions: **_fmalloc()**, **realloc()**, **calloc()**

> ```
> #include "malloc.h"
> ```
> ## char far *_fmalloc(size)
> **unsigned int size;**

The **_fmalloc()** function is not defined by the proposed ANSI standard. The **_fmalloc()** function returns a far pointer to the first byte of a region of memory of size *size* that has been allocated from outside the default data segment. If there is insufficient memory outside the default data segment, the heap will be tried. If both fail to satisfy the request, **_fmalloc()** returns a null pointer. It is always important to verify that the return value is not a null pointer before attempting to use it.

Related functions: **_ffree()**, **realloc()**, **calloc()**

> ```
> #include "stdlib.h" /* malloc.h in some systems */
> ```
> ## void free(ptr)
> **void *ptr;**

The **free()** function returns the memory pointed to by *ptr* back to the heap. This makes the memory available for future allocation.

It is imperative that **free()** only be called with a pointer that was previously allocated, using one of the dynamic allocation system's functions such as **malloc()** or **calloc()**. Using an invalid pointer in the call will probably destroy the memory-management mechanism and cause a system crash.

Related functions: **malloc()**, **realloc()**, **calloc()**

#include "malloc.h"
▶ **unsigned int _freect(size)**
unsigned int size;

The **_freect()** function is not defined by the proposed
ANSI standard. The **_freect()** function returns the approximate number of items of size *size* that can be allocated from the free memory left in the heap.

Related functions: **malloc()**, **_memavl()**

#include "malloc.h"
▶ **hfree(ptr);**
char far *ptr;

The **hfree()** function is not defined by the proposed ANSI
standard. The **hfree()** function returns the memory pointed
to by the far pointer *ptr* back to the system. This makes
the memory available for future allocation. The pointer
must have previously been allocated using **halloc()**.

It is imperative that **hfree()** only be called with a
pointer that was previously allocated using **halloc()**,
which is used to allocate blocks of memory greater than
64K. Using an invalid pointer in the call will probably
destroy the memory-management mechanism and cause
a system crash.

Related functions: **halloc()**, **realloc()**, **calloc()**, **mal-
loc()**

#include "malloc.h"
▶ **char far *halloc(num,size)**
long n;
unsigned int size;

The **halloc()** function is not defined by the proposed
ANSI standard. The **halloc()** function returns a far pointer
to the first byte of a region of memory of size *size*num*
that has been allocated from outside the default data

segment. That is, *num* objects of size *size* bytes will be allocated. If the allocation request fails due to insufficient free memory, **halloc()** returns a null pointer. It is always important to verify that the return value is not a null pointer before attempting to use it.

The **halloc()** function is used to allocate a block of memory larger than 64K on 8088 based computers.

#include "stdlib.h" /* malloc.h on some systems */
▶ **void *malloc(size)**
unsigned int size;

The **malloc()** function returns a pointer to the first byte of a region of memory of size *size* that has been allocated from the heap. If there is insufficient memory in the heap to satisfy the request, **malloc()** returns a null pointer. It is always important to verify that the return value is not a null pointer before attempting to use it. Attempting to use a null pointer will usually result in a system crash.

Related functions: **free()**, **realloc()**, **calloc()**

#include "malloc.h"
▶ **unsigned int _memavl()**

The **_memavl()** function is not defined by the proposed ANSI standard. The **_memavl()** function returns the approximate number of bytes of free memory left in the heap.

Related functions: **malloc()**, **free()**, **_freect()**

#include "malloc.h"
▶ **unsigned _msize(ptr)**
char *ptr;

The **_msize()** function is not defined by the proposed ANSI standard. The **_msize()** function returns the number of bytes in the allocated block of memory pointed to by *ptr*.

Related functions: **malloc()**, **realloc()**

#include "malloc.h"
void __nfree(ptr);
char near *ptr;

The __nfree() function is not defined by the proposed ANSI standard. The __nfree() function returns the memory pointed to by the near pointer *ptr* back to the system. This makes the memory available for future allocation. It is imperative that __nfree() only be called with a pointer that was previously allocated using __nmalloc(), which is used to allocate blocks of memory from the default data segment. Using an invalid pointer in the call will probably destroy the memory-management mechanism and cause a system crash.

Related functions: **halloc()**, **realloc()**, **calloc()**, **malloc()**

#include "malloc.h"
char near *__nmalloc(size)
unsigned int size;

The __nmalloc() function is not defined by the proposed ANSI standard. The __nmalloc() function returns a near pointer to the first byte of a region of memory of size *size* that has been allocated from inside the default data segment. This is only meaningful for programs that are compiled for the large model 8086 address mode and it allows the use of a 16-bit pointer. If the allocation request fails due to insufficient free memory, __nmalloc() returns a null pointer. It is always important to verify that the return value is not a null pointer before attempting to use it.

Related functions: __nfree(), **realloc()**, **calloc()**, **malloc()**

```
#include "stdlib.h"
/* malloc.h on many systems */
```
► **void *realloc(ptr, size)**
```
void *ptr;
unsized int size;
```

The **realloc()** function changes the size of the allocated memory pointed to by *ptr* to that specified by *size*. The value of *size* may be greater or less than the original. A pointer to the memory block is returned because it may be necessary for **realloc()** to move the block in order to increase its size. If this occurs, the contents of the old block are copied into the new block—no information is lost. If there is not enough free memory in the heap to allocate *size* bytes, then a null pointer is returned and the original block is freed (lost). This means that it is important to verify the success of a call to **realloc()**.

Related functions: **free()**, **malloc()**, **calloc()**

```
#include "malloc.h"
```
► **unsigned int stackavail()**

The **stackavail()** function is not defined by the proposed ANSI standard. The **stackavail()** function returns the approximate number of bytes that are available on the stack for allocation using **alloca()**.

A second and possibly more important use of **stackavail()** is as a predictor of possible heap-stack collisions that could be generated by recursive routines.

Related functions: **alloca()**, **_memavl()**, **_freect()**

MISCELLANEOUS FUNCTIONS

This chapter discusses all the standard functions that don't easily fit in any other category. They include various conversion, variable-length argument processing, sorting, and other functions.

Many of the functions covered here require the use of the header **stdlib.h**. According to the proposed ANSI standard, in this header are defined the two types **div_t** and **ldiv_t**, which are the types of the values returned by **div()** and **ldiv()**, respectively. These macros are also defined:

ERANGE: The value assigned to **errno** if a range error occurs.

HUGE_VAL: The largest value representable by the floating point routines.

RAND_MAX: The maximum value that can be returned by the **rand()** function.

Functions requiring different header files will be discussed in the following descriptions.

#include "stdlib.h"
▶ void abort()

The **abort()** function causes immediate termination of a program. Generally, no files are flushed. In environments that support it, **abort()** will return an implementation-defined value to the calling process (usually the operating system). The primary use of **abort()** is to prevent a runaway program from closing active files.

Related functions: **exit()**, **atexit()**

#include "stdlib.h"
▶ **int abs(num)**
int num;

The **abs()** function returns the absolute value of the integer *num*.

Related function: **labs()**

#include "assert.h"
▶ **void assert(exp)** /* exp is any valid C expression */

The **assert()** macro, defined in its header **assert.h**, writes error information to **stderr** and then aborts program execution if the expression *exp* evaluates to 0. Otherwise, **assert()** does nothing. Although the exact output is implementation defined, many compilers use a message similar to this:

Assertion failed: <expression>, file <file>, line <linenum>

The **assert()** macro is generally used to help verify that a program is operating correctly, with the expression being devised in such a way that it evaluates TRUE only when no errors have taken place.

It is not necessary to remove the **assert()** statements from the source code once a program is debugged; if the macro **NDEBUG** is defined (as anything), then the **assert()** macros will be ignored.

Related function: **abort()**

#include "stdlib.h"
▶ **int atexit(func)**
void (*func)();

The **atexit()** function establishes (registers) the function pointed to by *func* as the function to be called upon normal program termination. That is, at the end of a program run, the specified function will be called. The **atexit()** function returns 0 if the function is registered as the termination function, non-zero otherwise.

The proposed ANSI standard specifies that at least 32 termination functions may be established and that they will be called in the reverse order of their establishment—that is, the registration process is stacklike in nature.

Atexit() is sometimes called **onexit()** by compilers that have deviated slightly from the proposed standard.

Related functions: **exit()**, **abort()**

#include "stdlib.h"
▶ **double atof(str)**
    char *str;

The **atof()** function converts the string pointed to by *str* into a **double** value. The string must contain a valid floating point number. If this is not the case, the returned value is technically undefined; however, most implementations will return 0.

The number may be terminated by any character that cannot be part of a valid floating point number. This includes whitespace, punctuation (other than periods), and characters other than "E" or "e". This means that if **atof()** is called with "100.00HELLO", the value 100.00 will be returned.

Related functions: **atoi()**, **atol()**

#include "stdlib.h"
▶ **int atoi(str)**
    char *str;

The **atoi()** function converts the string pointed to by *str* into an **int** value. The string must contain a valid integer number. If this is not the case, the returned value is technically undefined; however, most implementations will return 0.

The number may be terminated by any character that

cannot be part of an integer number. This includes white-space, punctuation, and characters other than "E" or "e". This means that if **atoi**() is called with "123.23", the integer value 123 will be returned and the 0.23 ignored.

Related functions: **atof**(), **atol**()

```
#include "stdlib.h"
```
▶ **int atol(str)**
```
char *str;
```

The **atol**() function converts the string pointed to by *str* into a **long int** value. The string must contain a valid long integer number. If this is not the case, the returned value is technically undefined; however, most implementations will return 0.

The number may be terminated by any character that cannot be part of an integer number. This includes white-space, punctuation, and characters other than "E" or "e". This means that if **atol**() is called with "123.23", the integer value 123 will be returned and the 0.23 ignored.

Related functions: **atof**(), **atoi**()

```
#include "stdlib.h" /* search.h on some
                            systems */
```
▶ **void *bsearch(key, base, num, size, (compare))**
```
void *key, *base;
unsigned int num, size;
int (*compare)();
```

Most compilers that are not completely compatible with the proposed ANSI standard will substitute **char** pointers for the **void** pointer in the definition and use a type cast when working with other data types.

The **bsearch**() function performs a binary search on

the sorted array pointed to by *base* and returns a pointer to the first member that matches the key pointed to by *key.* The number of elements in the array is specified by *num* and the size (in bytes) of each element is described by *size*.

The function pointed to by *compare* is used to compare an element of the array with the key. The form of the *compare* function must be

```
func_name(arg1, arg2)
void *arg1, *arg2;
```

It must return the following values: If *arg1* is less than *arg2* then return less than 0. If *arg1* is equal to *arg2* then return 0. If *arg1* is greater than *arg2* then return greater than 0. The array must be sorted in scending order, with the lowest address containing the lowest element. If the array does not contain the key, then a null pointer is returned.

Related function: **qsort()**

▶
```
#include "stdlib.h"
```
void exit(status)
```
int status;
```

The **exit()** function causes immediate, normal termination of a program. The value of *status* is passed to the calling process, usually the operating system, if the environment supports it. By convention, if the value of *status* is 0, normal program termination is assumed. A non-zero value may be used to indicate an implementation-defined error.

Related functions: **atexit()**, **abort()**

#include "stdlib.h"
▶ div_t div(numer, denom)
int numer, denom;

The **div()** function returns the quotient and the remainder of the operation *numer/denom*. The structure type **div_t** is defined in **stdlib.h** and will have at least these two fields.

int quot; /* the quotient */
int rem; /* the remainder */

Related function: **ldiv()**

#include "stdlib.h"
▶ char *getenv(name)
char *name;

The **getenv()** function returns a pointer to environmental information associated with the string pointed to by *name* in the implementation-defined environmental information table. The string returned must never be changed by the program.

The environment of a program may include such things as path names and devices online. The exact nature of this data is implementation defined.

If a call is made to **getenv()** with an argument that does not match any of the environment data, a null pointer is returned.

Related function: **system()**

#include "stdlib.h"
▶ char *itoa(num, str, radix)
int num;
char *str;
int radix;

The **itoa()** function is not currently defined by the proposed ANSI standard. The **itoa()** function converts the integer *num* into its string equivalent and places the result in the string pointed to by *str*. The base of the output string is determined by *radix*, which may generally be in the range 2 through 16.

The **itoa()** function returns a pointer to *str*. Generally, there is no error return value. Be sure to call **itoa()** with a string of sufficient length to hold the converted result.

The main use of **itoa()** is to transform integers into strings so that they can be sent to a device not directly supported by the normal C I/O system—that is, a non-stream device. The same thing may be accomplished using **sprintf()**. The reason **itoa()** is included in this discussion is that its use is quite prevalent throughout older existing code.

Related functions: **atoi()**, **sscanf()**

▶
```
#include "stdlib.h"
long labs(num)
long num;
```

The **labs()** function returns the absolute value of the **long int** *num*.

Related function: **abs()**

▶
```
#include "stdlib.h"
ldiv_t ldiv(numer, denom)
long int numer, denom;
```

The **ldiv()** function returns the quotient and the remainder of the operation *numer/denom*.

The structure type **ldiv_t** is defined in **stdlib.h** and will have at least these two fields.

```
int quot; /* the quotient */
int rem; /* the remainder */
```

Related function: **div()**

```
#include "setjmp.h"
```
▶ **void longjmp(envbuf, val)**
```
jmp_buf envbuf;
int val;
```

The **longjmp()** instruction causes program execution to resume at the point of the last call to **setjmp()**. These two functions are C's way of providing for a jump between functions. Notice that the header **setjump.h** is required.

The **longjmp()** function operates by resetting the stack to that stored in *envbuf*, which must have been set by a prior call to **setjmp()**. This causes program execution to resume at the statement following the **setjmp()** invocation. That is, the computer is "tricked" into thinking that it never left the function that called **setjmp()**. (As a somewhat graphic explanation, the **longjmp()** function sort of "warps" across time and (memory) space to a previous point in your program without having to perform the normal function return process.)

The buffer *envbuf* is of type **jmp_buf**, which is defined in the header **setjmp.h**. The buffer must have been set through a call to **setjmp()** prior to calling **longjmp()**.

The value of *val* becomes the return value of **setjump()** and may be interrogated to determine where the long jump came from. The only value not allowed is 0.

It is important to understand that the **longjmp()** function must be called before the function that called **setjmp()** returns. If not, the result is technically undefined. (Actually, a crash will almost certainly occur.)

By far the most common use of **longjmp()** is to return from a deeply nested set of routines when a catastrophic error occurs.

Related function: **setjmp()**

#include "stdlib.h"
▶ char *ltoa(num, str, radix)
int long num;
char *str;
int radix;

The **ltoa()** function is not currently defined by the proposed ANSI standard. The **ltoa()** function converts the
long integer *num* into its string equivalent and places the
result in the string pointed to by *str*. The base of the
output string is determined by *radix*, which may generally
be in the range 2 through 16.

The **ltoa()** function returns a pointer to *str*. Generally,
there is no error return value. Be sure to call **ltoa()** with
a string of sufficient length to hold the converted result.

The main use of **ltoa()** is to transform integers into
strings so that they can be sent to a device that is not
directly supported by the normal C I/O system—that is,
a non-stream device. The same thing may be accomplished using **sprintf()**. **ltoa()** is included in this discussion because its use is quite prevalent throughout older
existing code.

Related functions: **itoa()**, **sscanf()**

#include "stdio.h" /* stdlib.h in some systems */
▶ void perror(str)
char *str;

The **perror()** function maps the value of the global **errno**
onto a string and writes that string to **stderr**. If the value
of *str* is not null, then the string is written first, followed
by a colon and then by the proper error message.

```
#include "stdlib.h" /* search.h on some
                        systems */
```

► **void qsort(base, num, size,
    (compare))**
```
void *base;
unsigned int num, size;
int (*compare)();
```

Most compilers that are not completely compatible with the proposed ANSI standard will substitute **char** pointers instead of **void** pointers, and will use an explicit type cast for other data types.

The **qsort()** function sorts the array pointed to by *base* using a quicksort (developed by C.A.R. Hoare). The quicksort is generally considered the best general-purpose sorting algorithm. Upon termination, the array will be sorted. The number of elements in the array is specified by *num*, and the size (in bytes) of each element is described by *size*.

The function pointed to by *compare* is used to compare an element of the array with the key. The form of the *compare* function must be:

```
func_name(arg1, arg2)
void *arg1, *arg2;
```

It must return the following values: If *arg1* is less than *arg2* then return less than 0. If *arg1* is equal to *arg2* then return 0. If *arg1* is greater than *arg2* then return greater than 0. The array is sorted into ascending order, with the lowest address containing the lowest element.

Related function: **bsearch()**

```
#include "signal.h"
```
► **int raise(signal)**
```
int signal;
```

The **raise()** function sends the signal specified by *signal* to an executing program. This implies a multitasking envi

ronment. It returns zero if successful, non-zero otherwise.
Related function: **signal()**

#include "stdlib.h"
▶ int rand()

The **rand()** function generates a sequence of pseudo-random numbers. Each time it is called an integer between 0 and **RAND_MAX** is returned.
Related function: **srand()**

#include "setjmp.h"
▶ int setjmp(envbuf)
jmp_buf envbuf;

The **setjmp()** function saves the contents of the system stack in the buffer *envbuf* for later use by **longjmp()**.

The **setjmp()** function returns 0 upon invocation. However, a **longjmp()** passes an argument to **setjmp()** when it executes, and it is this value (always non-zero) that will appear to be **setjmp()**'s value after a call to **longjmp()**.
Related function: **longjmp()**

#include "signal.h"
▶ void (*signal(signal, func)()
int signal; /* int */
void (*func)()

The **signal()** function defines the function, *func*, to be executed if the specified signal *signal* is received. The operation of this function is somewhat implementation-specific. However, the following discussion will give you

121

a rough idea of its operation. The value of *sig* may be any one of the following macros that are defined in **signal.h**:

Macro	Meaning
SIGABRT	abort termination
SIGFPE	detect errors in arithmetic
SIGILL	detect an invalid function
SIGINT	detect a system interrupt
SIGSEGV	detect invalid memory access
SIGTERM	detect an external termination request

The value for *func* must be one of the following macros, defined in **signal.h**, or the address of a function.

Macro	Meaning
SIG_DFL	use default signal handling
SIG_IGN	ingore the signal

If a function address is used, the specified function will be executed.

Related function: **raise()**

#include "stdlib.h"
▶ **void srand(seed)**
  unsigned int seed;

The **srand()** function is used to set a starting point for the sequence generated by **rand()**. (The **rand()** function returns pseudo-random numbers.) **Srand()** is generally used to allow multiple program runs, using different sequences of pseudo-random numbers.

Related function: **rand()**

```
#include "stdlib.h"
```
▶ **double strtod(start, end)**
```
char *start;
char **end;
```

The **strtod()** function converts the string representation
of a number stored in the string pointed to by *start* into
a **double** and returns the result.

The **strtod()** function works as follows. First, any
whitespace in the string pointed to by *start* is stripped.
Next, each character that comprises the number is read.
Any character that cannot be part of a floating point
number will cause this process to stop. This includes
whitespace, punctuation (other than periods), and characters other than "E" or "e". Finally, *end* is set to point to
the remainder, if any, of the original string. This means
that if **strtod()** is called with " 100.00 Pliers", the value
100.00 will be returned and *end* will point to the space
that precedes "Pliers."

If a conversion error occurs, **strtod()** returns either
HUGE_VAL for overflow, or − **HUGE_VAL** for underflow. If no conversion could take place, then 0 is returned.

Related function: **atof()**

```
#include "stdlib.h"
```
▶ **long int strtol(start, end, radix)**
```
char *start;
char **end;
int radix
```

The **strtol()** function converts the string representation
of a number stored in the string pointed to by *start* into
a **long int** and returns the result. The base of the number
is determined by *radix*. If *radix* is zero, the base is determined by rules that govern constant specification. If the
radix is other than zero, then it must be in the range 2
through 36.

The **strtol()** function works as follows. First, any whitespace in the string pointed to by *start* is stripped. Next, each character that comprises the number is read. Any character that cannot be part of a long integer number will cause this process to stop. This includes whitespace, punctuation, and characters. Finally, *end* is set to point to the remainder, if any, of the original string. This means that if **strtol()** is called with " 100 Pliers", the value 100L will be returned and end will point to the space that precedes "Pliers."

If a conversion error occurs, **strtol()** returns either **LONG_MAX** for overflow, or **LONG_MIN** for underflow. If no conversion could take place, then 0 is returned.

Related function: **atol()**

```
#include "stdlib.h"
```
▶ **unsigned long int strtoul(start, end, radix)**
```
char *start;
char **end;
int radix;
```

The **strtoul()** function converts the string representation of a number stored in the string pointed to by *start* into an **unsigned long int** and returns the result. The base of the number is determined by *radix*. If *radix* is zero, the base is determined by rules that govern constant specification. If the radix is specified, it must be in the range 2 through 36.

The **strtoul()** function works as follows. First, any whitespace in the string pointed to by start is stripped. Next, each character that comprises the number is read. Any character that cannot be part of an unsigned long integer number will cause this process to stop. This includes whitespace, punctuation, and characters. Finally, *end* is set to point to the remainder, if any, of the original string. This means that if **strtoul()** is called with " 100

Pliers", the value 100L will be returned and *end* will point to the space that precedes "Pliers."

If a conversion error occurs, **strtoul()** returns either **ULONG_MAX** for overflow, or **ULONG_MIN** for underflow. If no conversion could take place, then 0 is returned.

Related function: **strtol()**

```
#include "stdlib.h"
```
▶ **int system(str)**
    char *str

The **system()** function passes the string pointed to by *str* as a command to the command processor of the operating system. If **system()** is called with a null pointer it will return non-zero if a *command processor* is present, 0 otherwise. (Remember, some C code will be executed in dedicated systems that do not have operating systems and command processors.) The proposed ANSI standard states that the return value of **system()** when called with a string is implementation defined. However, generally it will return 0 if the command was successfully executed, non-zero otherwise.

Related function: **exit()**

```
#include "stdarg.h"
```
▶ **void va_arg(argptr, last_parm)**
    va_list argptr;
    last_parm; /* type unknown until time of call */
▶ **void va_end(argptr)**
    va_list argptr;
▶ **va_arg(argptr, type)**
    va_list argptr;
    type; /* type is unknown until time of call */

The macros **va_arg()** and **va_start()** and the function **va_end()** work together to allow a variable number of arguments to be passed to a function. The most common example of a function that takes a variable number of arguments is **printf()**. The type **va_list** is defined by **stdarg.h**.

The general procedure for creating a function that can take a variable number of arguments is as follows. The function must have at least one known parameter, but may have more, prior to the variable parameter list. The right-most known parameter is called the *last_parm*. Before any of the variable length parameters may be accessed, the argument pointer *argptr* must be initialized through a call to **va_start()**. After that, parameters are returned via calls to **va_arg()**, with *type* being the type of the next parameter. Finally, once all the parameters have been read and prior to returning from the function, a call to **va_end()** must be made to ensure that the stack is properly restored. If **va_end()** is not called, a program crash is very likely.

Related function: **vprintf()**